Table of Contents

TRADEMARKS AND COPYRIGHT

AirsoftPRESS.com (a.k.a. AirsoftPRESS) is an independent content developer. We at AirsoftPRESS are not associated nor affiliated with the firearm/airsoft replica manufacturer(s) mentioned in this book. The name(s), model(s) and other specific properties of the firearm(s)/replica(s) mentioned in this book are the trademark(s) of the respective manufacturer(s). We mention these name(s) and/or the relevant terminologies only for describing the relevant Airsoft technical knowledge (i.e. Fair Use).

Our publications are fully copyrighted. Unauthorized re-production or duplication are strictly prohibited.

AirsoftPRESS will not be held liable for any advice or suggestions given in this book. If the reader wants to follow a suggestion, it is at his or her own discretion. Suggestions are only offered to help.

ABOUT THE REAL STEEL

The Dragunov sniper rifle was a squad support weapon designed to provide long-range engagement ability. It was invented in the Sovient Union, with licensed production eventually established in China and Iran. Technically it is a semi-automatic rifle that has a short-stroke gas-piston system, a relatively thin barrel profile ended with a slotted flash suppressor, a two-piece wooden handguard and a wooden thumbhole stock.

PREFACE

This training book has been developed from the ground up for beginners who know little about Airsoft sniper rifle technology. As part of our Airsoft Technology Self-Paced Training Series, this book gives an introduction to the SVD Sniper with Co-2 upgrade architecture. The primary goal of this book is to explain the various technical concepts in very simple language.

We believe that this book and its support materials have everything you need for an informative, interesting, challenging and entertaining Airsoft educational experience.

We use the Dragunov SVD sniper rifle from a Chinese manufacturer for demonstration. The real steel Dragunov is a semi-automatic sniper rifle developed in the Soviet Union. Surprisingly, it was not meant for specialized sniper teams but rather for designated marksmen spread in basic infantry units.

You are encouraged to think about the significance of performance difference brought about by an upgrade. Based on our experience and observation, a FPS increase of approx. 40~50 does make a visible difference when the total FPS before upgrade is under 300. That is, a Springer running at 340 does give better result in a visible manner then one running at 290. However, the marginal gain tends to fall as you move up the FPS curve - you cannot really tell a practical difference between 340 and 380 UNLESS you are also moving up to 0.3g or 0.4g BBs, which may be way too heavy for Springers. Frankly, difference in meter reading does not always translate into difference in real world effectiveness.

When you do your upgrade, there is really no need to go for a certain FPS level very precisely (unless you are selling your services). Someone 80 feet away will tell you that he feels the same when being shot at 320 and 340. Using CO-2 is different – the room for power increase is huge (although you may risk breaking your local law).

FYI: When you shoot a 450FPS airsoft in a public place where the power limit is only 350, you break the law and may be fined or sentenced as a result. When you shoot a 300FPS airsoft in a public place where the power limit is 350 and that a car's window is broken, you may break the law as your action has actually produced risk and damage on other's property, NOT because of any power limit issue. You may be fined or sentenced as a result. You will still need to compensate the car owner for the damage produced.

By the way, in addition to FPS, it is suggested that you also consider your gun's hitting power (i.e. the impact). Heavy BBs drag down FPS (due to the heavier weight) but may produce higher impact (also due to the heavier weight). What this indicates is that FPS rating alone may not truly reflect how powerful a Springer is.

While FPS measurement (feet per second) looks primarily at the "speed" of the flying bullet (i.e. the muzzle velocity)(!), Joule measurement (a system commonly in use in the UK) does take bullet weight into the equation to more accurately measure the force generated (i.e. the impact energy). In fact, we at The AirsoftPRESS prefer Joule measurement over FPS. However, it seems like the market in North America is biased totally towards the FPS system.

Using Speed Tester (Ball bullet shooting chronograph)

The speed tester shown above is a XCortech X3200. It is a simple device. As you can see from the picture below, the bullet passes through two checkpoints and the speed is accordingly measured.

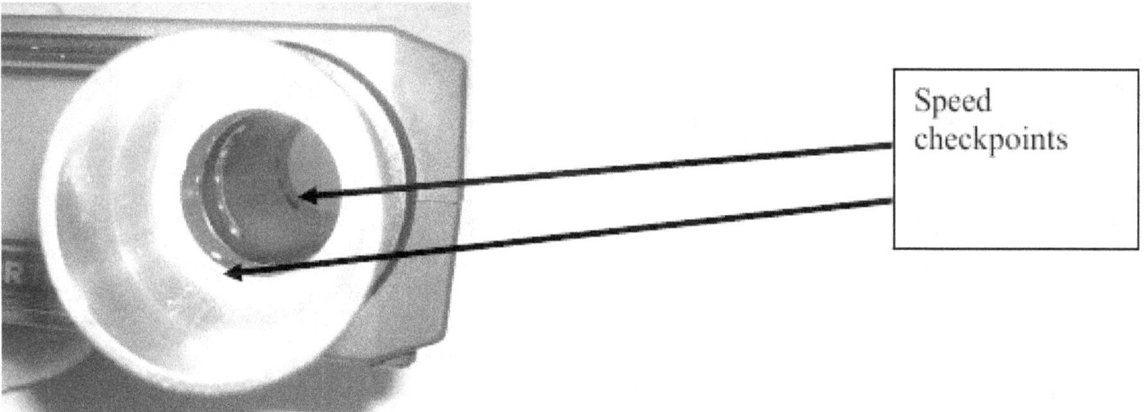

Results will be shown on the small display screen at the front of the device.

BACKGROUND CONCEPT ON THE ORIGINAL COCKING MECHANISM

A springer functions by the cocking handle (or the slide if the gun is a hand gun, or the pump if the gun is a shot gun) carrying the piston, holding a spring against the frame and to a catch which holds it in a compressed state.

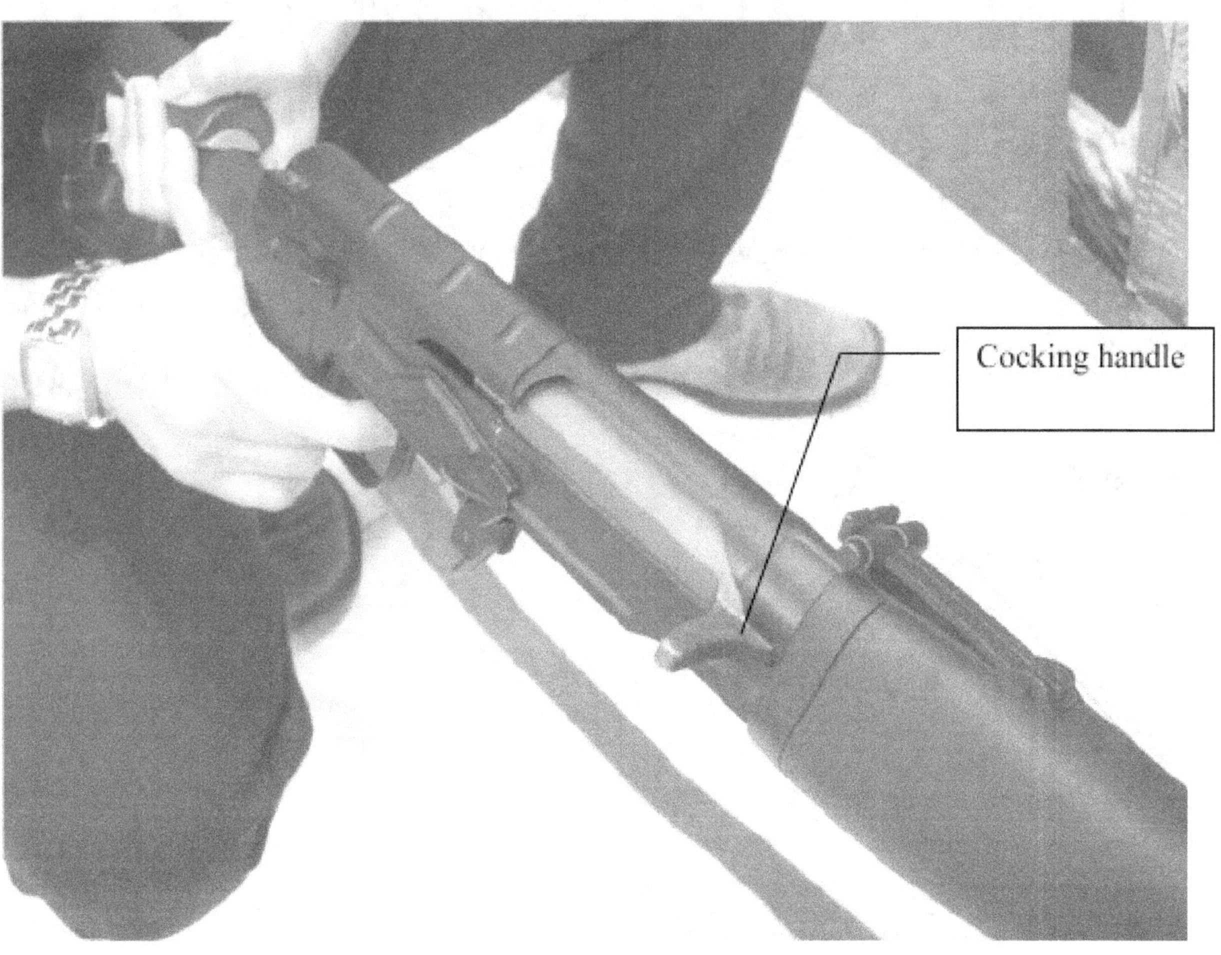

When you pull the trigger, the catch is released and the spring is decompressed. The piston is being pushed forward towards the cylinder. Compressed air is produced, causing the BB bullet to accelerate down the barrel.

This selector switch is only for safe and single shot. When you put it in the safe position, the charging handle will not be able to go far enough back to properly cock the spring.

FYI, the Springer cycling mechanism provides the basis for AEGs (Automatic Electric Guns), which are fully automatic in the cocking process - the cocking action is implemented through a motor driven mechbox without the need for manual intervention.

		

Since the cycling process is entirely manual, comfortable cocking is a factor that must be considered if you choose to stay with the spring powered mechanism!

There has been a myth around saying that a very long spring is a MUST for delivering higher FPS. **This is not always true.** On every compression spring there are several parameters. The "free length" is the length of a spring with no load applied. "Length before set" can be thought of as near the maximum compressed length of a spring (let's refer to this as the compressed length). The number of coils also plays a role in determining the strength of a spring.

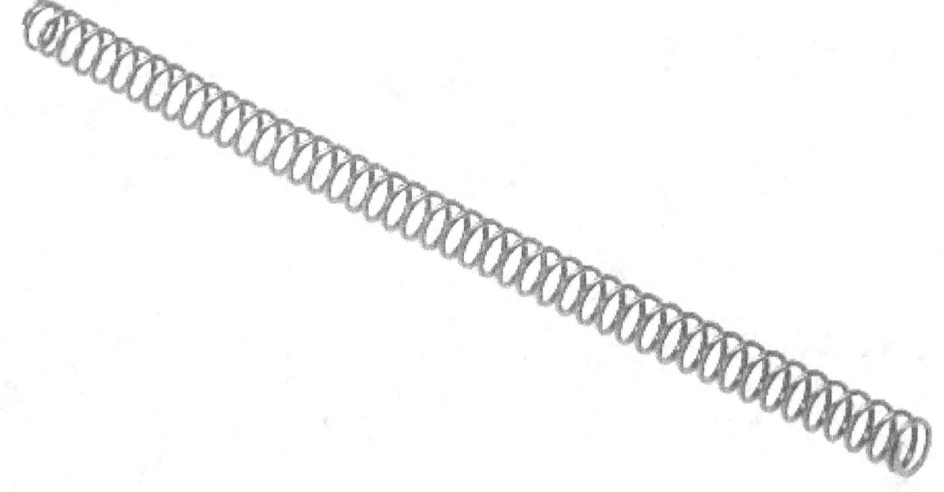

Generally speaking, the more coils a spring has the more powerful it is. However, the material that is used for producing the spring and the corresponding heat treatment process are even more critical. Put it this way, a soft spring with 10 coils may well be "weaker" than a hard spring with 5 coils. Also, not all coils are active (this apply especially to variable-pitch springs). And, installation-wise, a spring that is too long (a high free-length parameter) is much harder to fit into the gun.

A softer but longer spring does have an advantage over a shorter but harder spring. A softer spring imposes less initial load while cocking. A harder spring may make it very difficult to cock by hand.

When you cock the gun, the piston is pushed all the way back until it can get in touch with the tail of the catch. If the upgrade spring at full compression is too lengthy, the piston will never be able to reach the desired position. This is why you need to be very careful when selecting an upgrade spring. Also check the diameter of the spring wire. If the spring wire has a large diameter, the compressed length may be too long. Also pay attention to the number of coils. A short spring with MANY coils can be very lengthy even at full compression.

When you want to put a spacer on the spring guide (for increasing the compression effect), always ensure that the spacer is of a suitable diameter. If your spacer has an outside diameter exceeding the inside diameter of the piston and that the spacer is too thick, the piston's backward movement will be blocked. Even if your spacer has a piston-safe diameter, use it very carefully. The use of additional spacer is no different from using a spring that is too long. If spacer is used inside the piston (rather than with the spring guide), make sure the spring guide won't hit the spacer during full compression. In any case, we found that using spacer for better FPS is effective and safe only for harder and shorter springs. On softer springs the small increase in FPS has no real world significance at all.

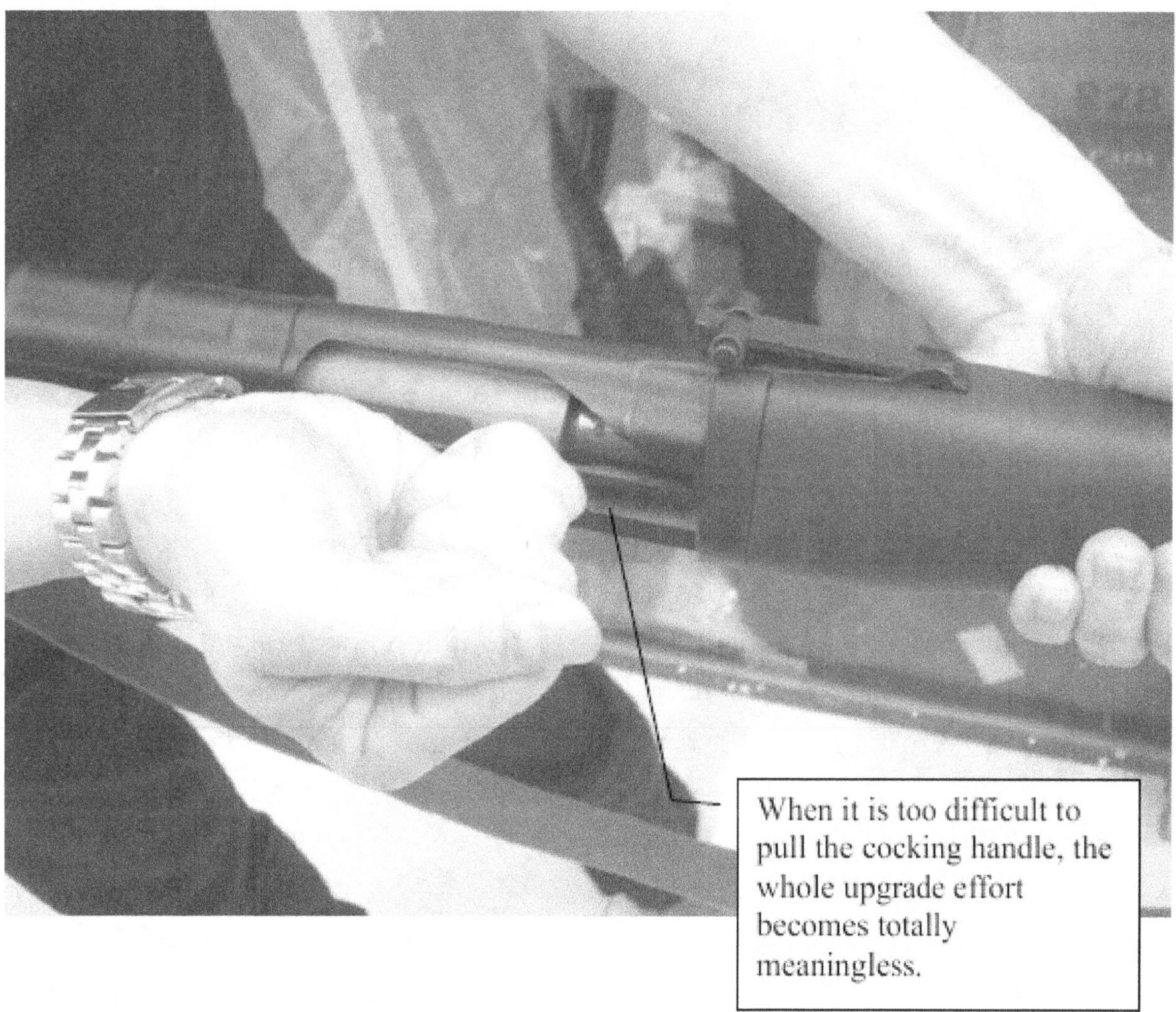

When it is too difficult to pull the cocking handle, the whole upgrade effort becomes totally meaningless.

The pitch of a spring refers to the distance, center to center, between two coils. A variable-pitch spring is one that starts out "soft" and after a certain load is placed on it, becomes stiffer. This kind of design is good if you want smoother and less exhaustive cocking. The technology involved in creating such a spring is not rocket-science. When you've wound what you want at the first pitch, simply stop the lathe and change the lead screw speed setting to the second position. Continue winding at the second pitch until you want to change the pitch again.

A long variable-pitched spring:

When looking at a variable pitch spring, also pay attention to the number of active coils. Active coils are coils which contribute to the motive force of the spring. Only the coils which show daylight between them are active coils. Non-active coils usually act as spacer and nothing else.

Occasionally you may need to cut a spring to make it fits into your Springer. If you do so, make sure to ground the spring on both ends. Grinding is the process of grounding the ends of a spring. Springs found in good quality springers are usually grounded, which look highly professional. Generally speaking, when a spring is ground on both ends, it can spin more freely during compression. Why is it necessary for the spring to spin? By allowing the spring to spin, less stress is imposed on the internals and cocking can be made a little easier.

The quality of a spring depends largely on the built material as well as the workmanship of the spring shop. If you go to a good spring shop, chance is that you can get a tailor made spring as good as those offered by Systema and PDI.

The Systema/PDI springs are originally designed for AEGs. However, they can be used in your Springers as well (as long as the sizes fit). If you buy a Systema (or PDI) spring, you know at the time of purchase what FPS can be approximately achieved. Their products are proven. With a custom made spring, you must measure the FPS and may have to do fine tuning on your own.

Systema springs are in general longer and harder, while PDI springs are shorter and a little softer. Both of them are from Japan and are of similar prices. People prefer PDI springs because PDI springs are thought to be less stressful for the gears.

Based on our experience, both of them are OK. Below is a table for your reference. Note that the FPS figures were measured on AEGs – with Springers the figures will likely vary (based on our experience, expect 10~15% less in performance when using these springs on a Springer due to the fact Springers in general are not as good in terms of air sealing):

Systema	PDI approx. equivalence	FPS with 0.20g BBs
M90	100%	295~300
M100	120%	325~340
M110	150%	365~380
M120	170%	390~400
M130	210%	425~440

LIMITATIONS OF THE ORIGINAL COCKING MECHANISM

Whether an upgrade objective is realistic or not depends largely on the foundation – how solid is your stock gun? With an upgrade spring in place, both the piston and the cylinder are directly affected by increased impact. However, their round tube shapes make reinforcement highly difficult.

When you install a very stiff spring, the piston may break easily. In Japan, expert gunsmiths like to tailor make metal reinforcement parts. We have seen someone reinforcing a cylinder by putting in a custom made metal tube. This add-on metal tube "eats" a significant portion of the increased impact force.

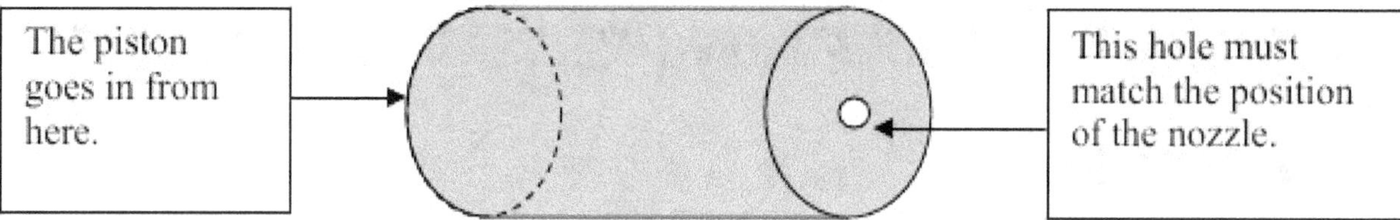

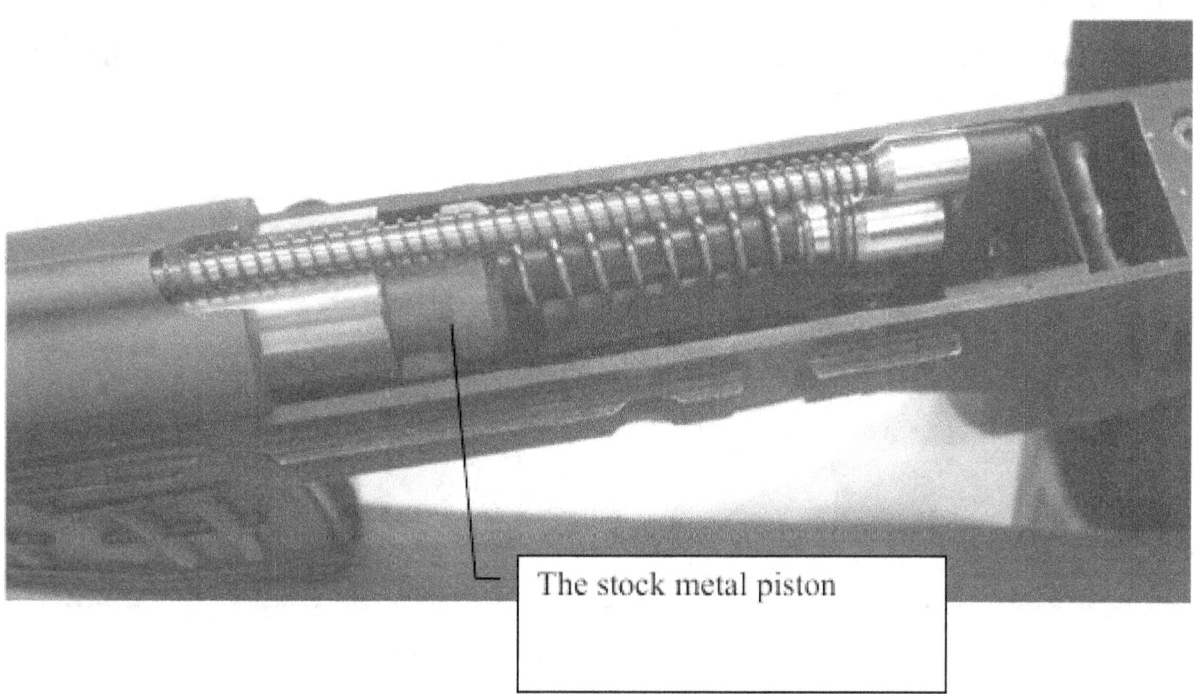

The cocking handle / cocking tube may break when you cock hard. In fact handle breakage is pretty common on guns using cheap recycled metal material. Sadly there is not much you can do about it.

BACKGROUND CONCEPT ON PRECISION AND RANGE IMPROVEMENT

High precision INNER barrel helps increase both the muzzle velocity and the accuracy of a gun by reducing the inner diameter. Most high precision barrels are highly polished on the inside (nickel-plated and teflon coated) for minimizing wear and tear.

Potential problems with a larger diameter barrel:

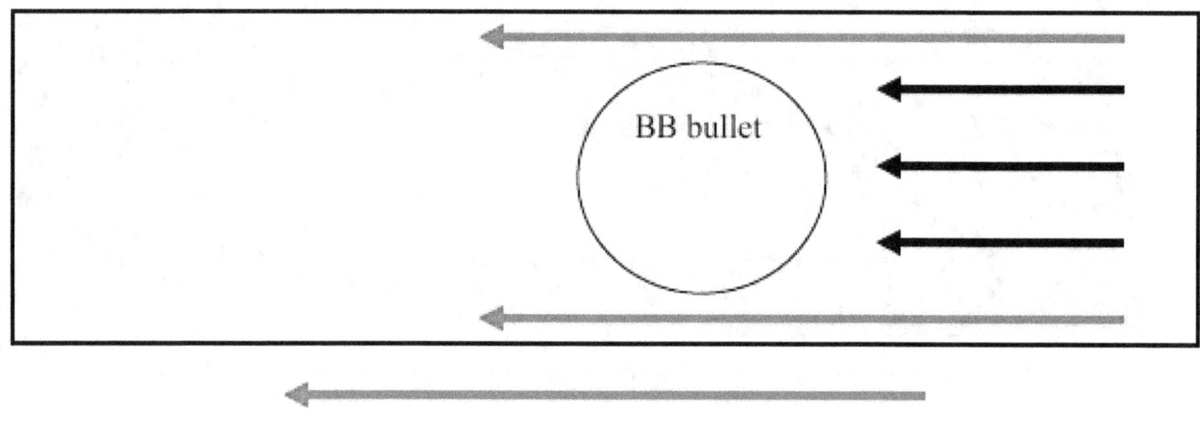

Energy that has been wasted.

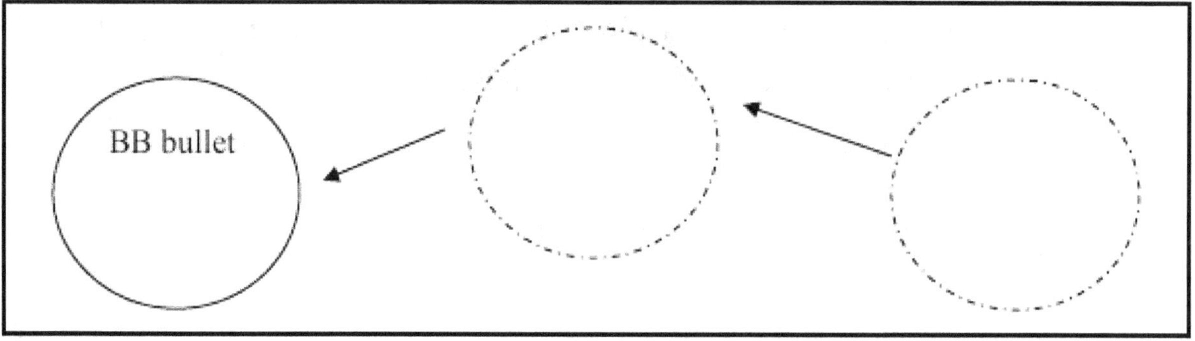

The majority of high precision barrels in the market are for use by AEGs. However, most of the time you will be able to find an AEG barrel that works for your Springer diameter-wise. Length-wise, minor modification may be necessary.

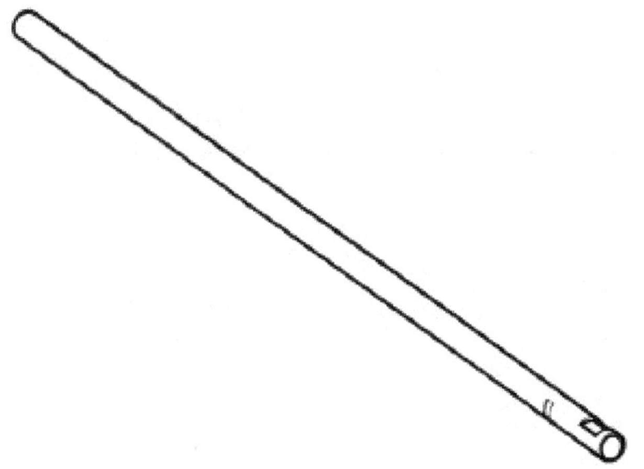

If you choose to create your own high precision barrel, you will also need to create your own hopup function.

This is NOT an option suitable for beginners. Only an expert gunsmith would have the skills and tools necessary for creating his own tailor-made barrel.

Refer to the illustration below, you need to first make a small opening on the upper side of the barrel.

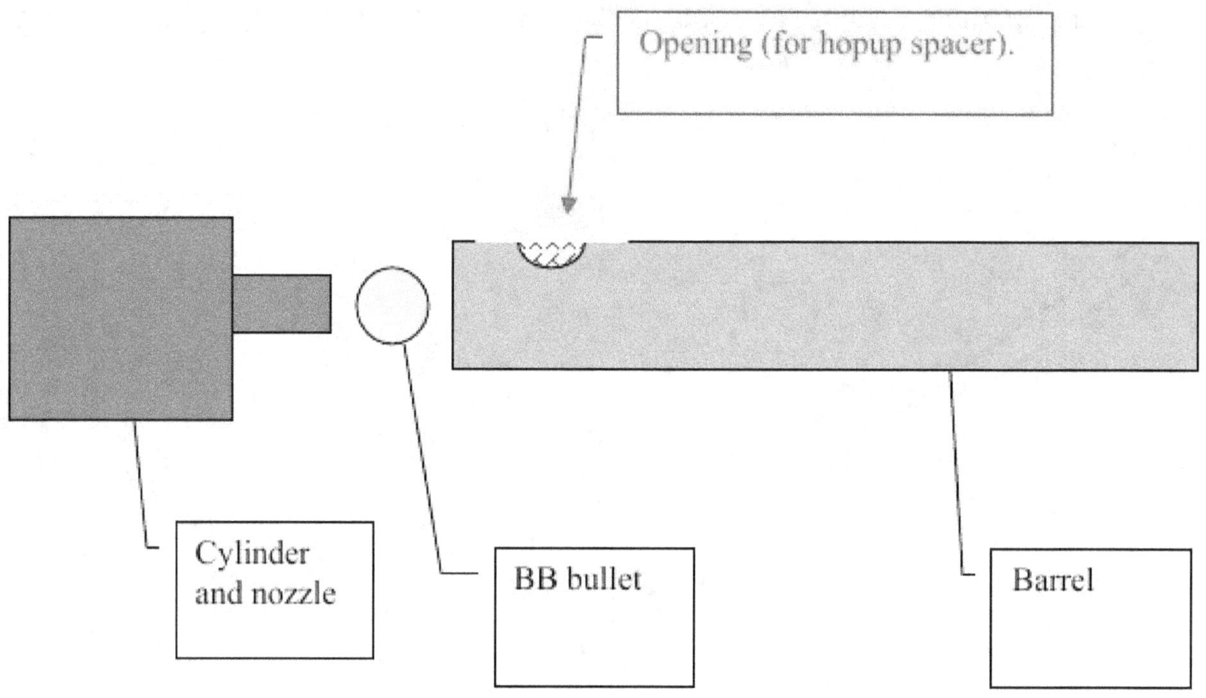

Have a small piece of rubber tube ready for use with the barrel (see below):

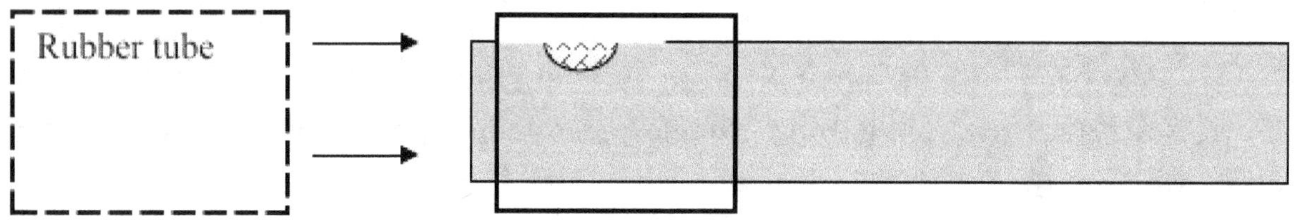

Place a small screw on the rubber tube (right on top of the position of the barrel opening). You do NOT want to screw through the rubber tube. Add a small rubber pad in between to serve as a spacer (the "bucking"). Finally, secure the screw to make it firmly attached to the barrel:

You should test the hopup unit with high quality 0.20g or 0.25g BB bullets. Do understand that different BBs react differently to the hopup effect, and minor adjustment made be necessary if you want the bullets to have a straight flight path.

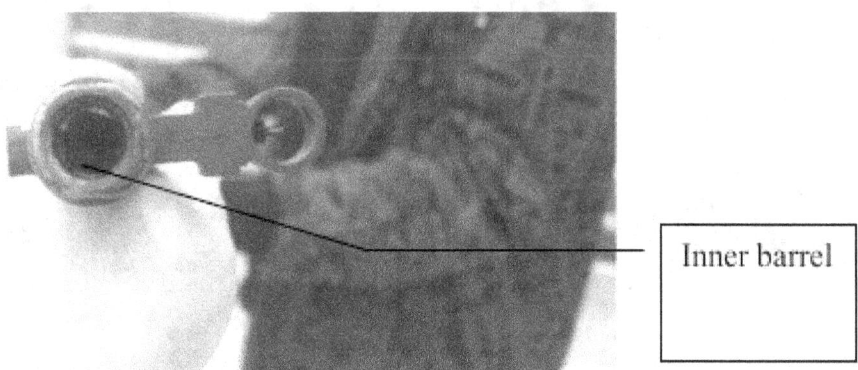

Do understand that a high precision barrel has very little tolerance on dust and dirt, and is not recommended for outdoor use. In fact, high precision barrel in general has an inner diameter too small to accommodate dirt and poor quality BBs. To avoid jamming, you must do whatever you can do to keep the barrel completely clean and properly lubed. You must use the best BBs, and must keep the magazine very clean (so that no dirt can ever get attached to the BBs).

A high precision barrel also demands the use of very high quality BBs. There is currently a wide range of BBs out there in the market that varies in quality. So which one should you use? In fact, one most obvious quality indicator is the bullet shape and finishing. A high quality BB bullet will always be a perfect sphere with no imperfections or mold lines.

High precision barrel primarily addresses the concern on accuracy.

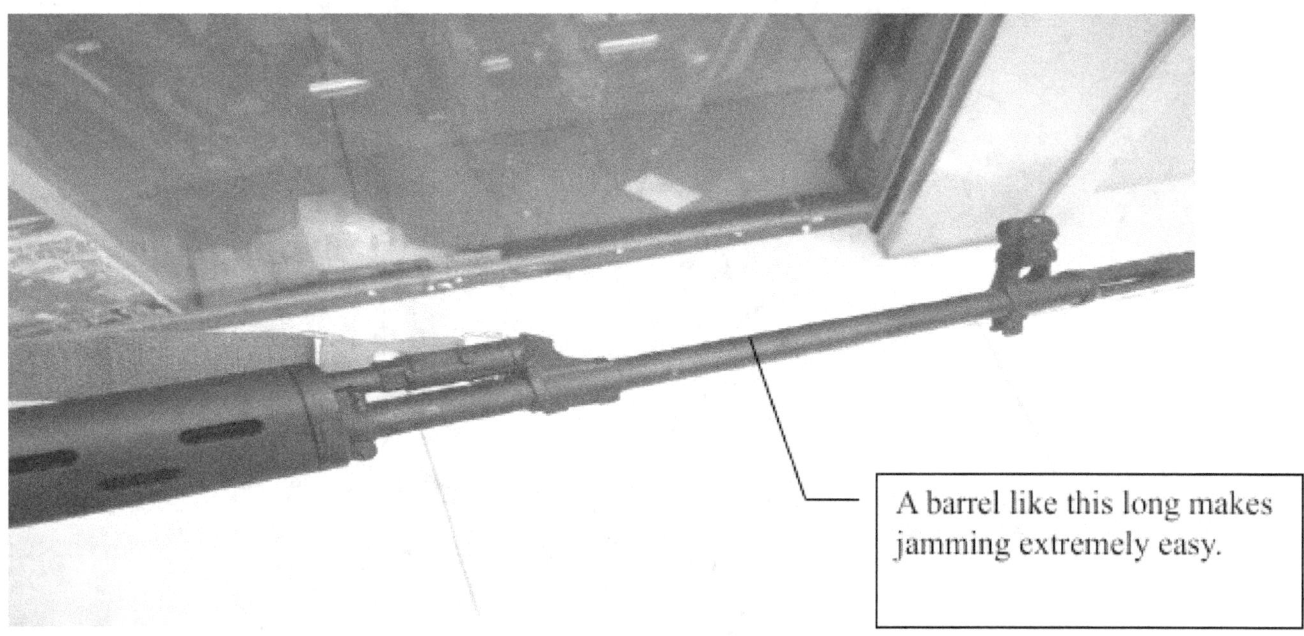

FYI, the stock magazine is a unique high capacity magazine which is only compatible with the Dragunovs and nothing else. It is NOT AK compatible.

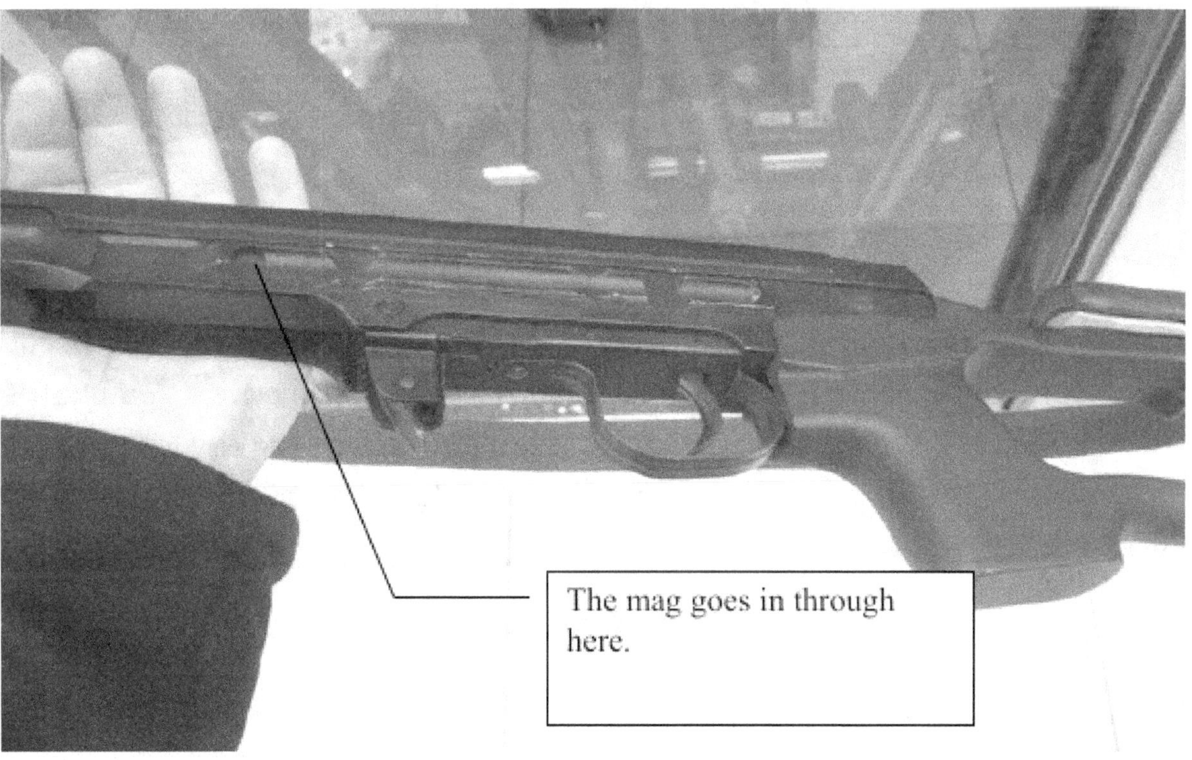

Range improvement is achieved primarily through implementing the hopup back spinning mechanism. According to the Bernoulli's principle, if a bullet is given a backspin an overpressure is formed under the bullet and an underpressure is formed on the top of the bullet. The bullet is therefore sucked up - this is why it can fly farther.

<u>Refer to the diagram below:</u>

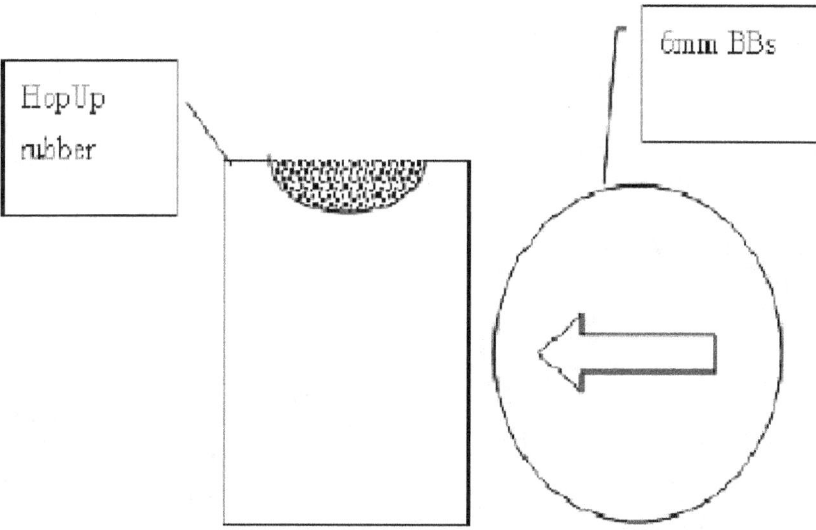

When a BB bullet travels through the barrel, the downward tip of the hopup rubber touches the bullet and makes it back-spin. Do note that if the BB has a size which is too big or too small, the hopup unit will not be able to generate the necessary friction on it. Also, if the hopup rubber is not properly maintained, it will gradually get worn out to an extent that hopup is no longer effective. Generally speaking, the rubber should be replaced after about 13000~15000 shots.

The best way to maintain the hopup rubber is to properly lube it after each game. Do NOT use WD-40. Use silicon oil spray, and use it AFTER (not before) each game (lubrication can lead to unstable bullet flight path).

In fact, you should also use silicon oil spray for barrel cleaning - you spray and then use a cleaning rod to clean the inside of the barrel. This can remove any dirt accumulated and can greatly reduce the likelihood of bullet jamming.

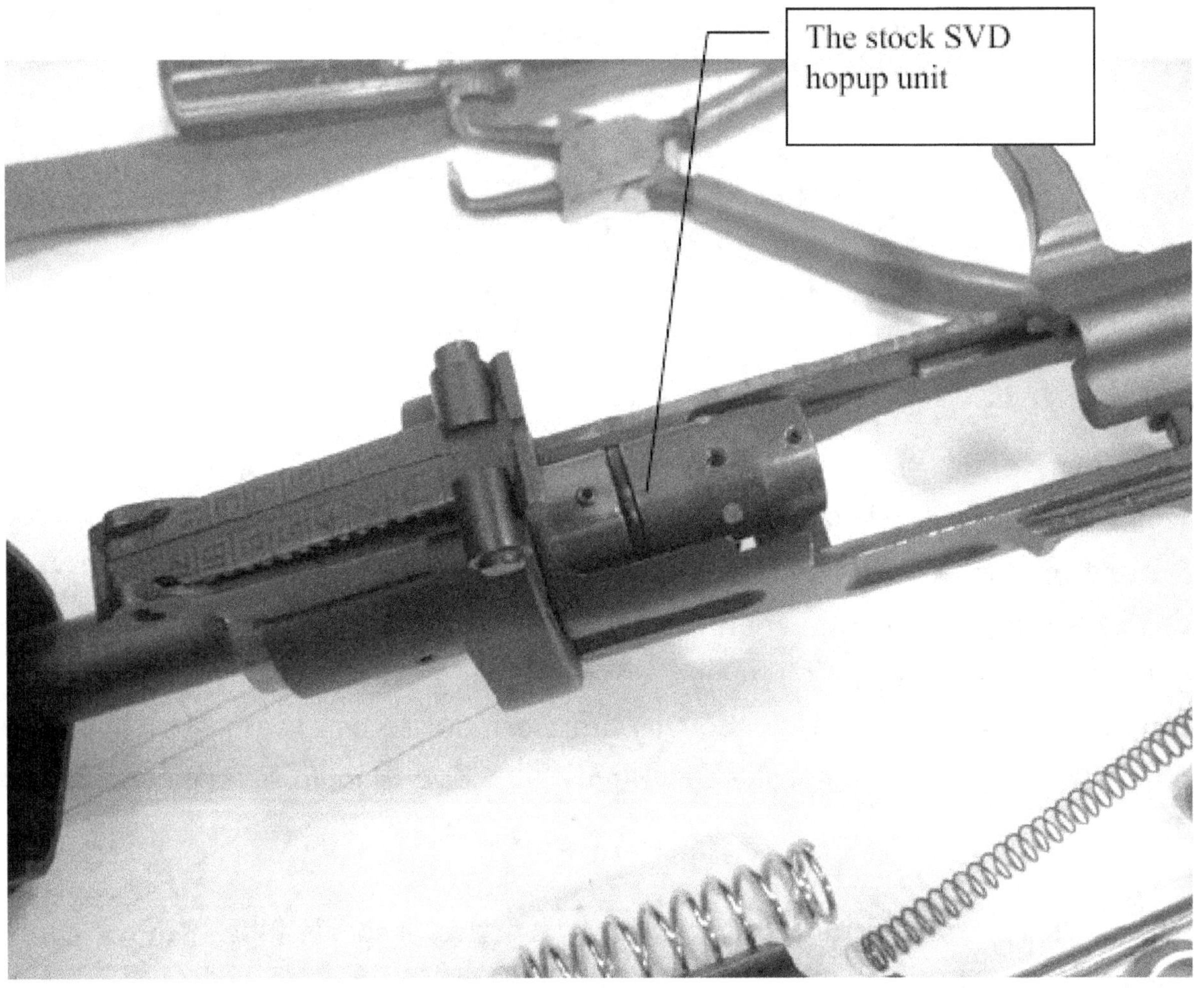

If your gun already has a functional hopup unit built-in but the back spinning effect is too weak, chance is that the hopup was originally calibrated for supporting light weight BBs. To improve the hopup effect, you will need to replace the original hopup spacer (i.e. the bucking) with a thicker one. It is trial and error on getting the right size - you may have to do this a couple of times.

If your hopup does not produce the desired effect, chance is that the hopup spacer (bucking) is too soft. You may save $ by using simple quick fixes. For example, to "harden" the spacer a little bit, you may insert a small piece of electric wire into it so the space inside is effectively filled up. Or, you can use the ink tube inside a pen as a cheap replacement. You just have to look for one with identical dimension.

Regardless of what you do with the hop spacer, always perform a visual check by looking through the inside of the barrel. If the hop bucking sticks too far into the barrel, your gun will shoot the sky. You don't want this to happen.

Keep in mind that friction must exist for hopup to work. If the barrel is over-lubed, there will be no friction and thus no back spinning. Double feeding may occur when the feeding mechanism is over lubricated or when the nozzle is seriously deformed. It may also occur with improper cocking behavior (which is basically a user error).

Double feeding refers to the feeding of two (or more) BBs at once. Double feeding may result in both BBs breaking or serious jamming in the barrel. Even if the BBs do not break, their range and accuracy may be greatly reduced.

BASIC CONCEPT OF CO-2 UPGRADE

The heart of the CO2 upgrade is a special cylinder/piston set (AKA reservoir chamber or pressure accumulation chamber). The CO2 cartridge is housed in a special "piston". The original cocking mechanism is retained for "activating" the CO2 mechanism. Shooting requires cocking on a per shot basis.

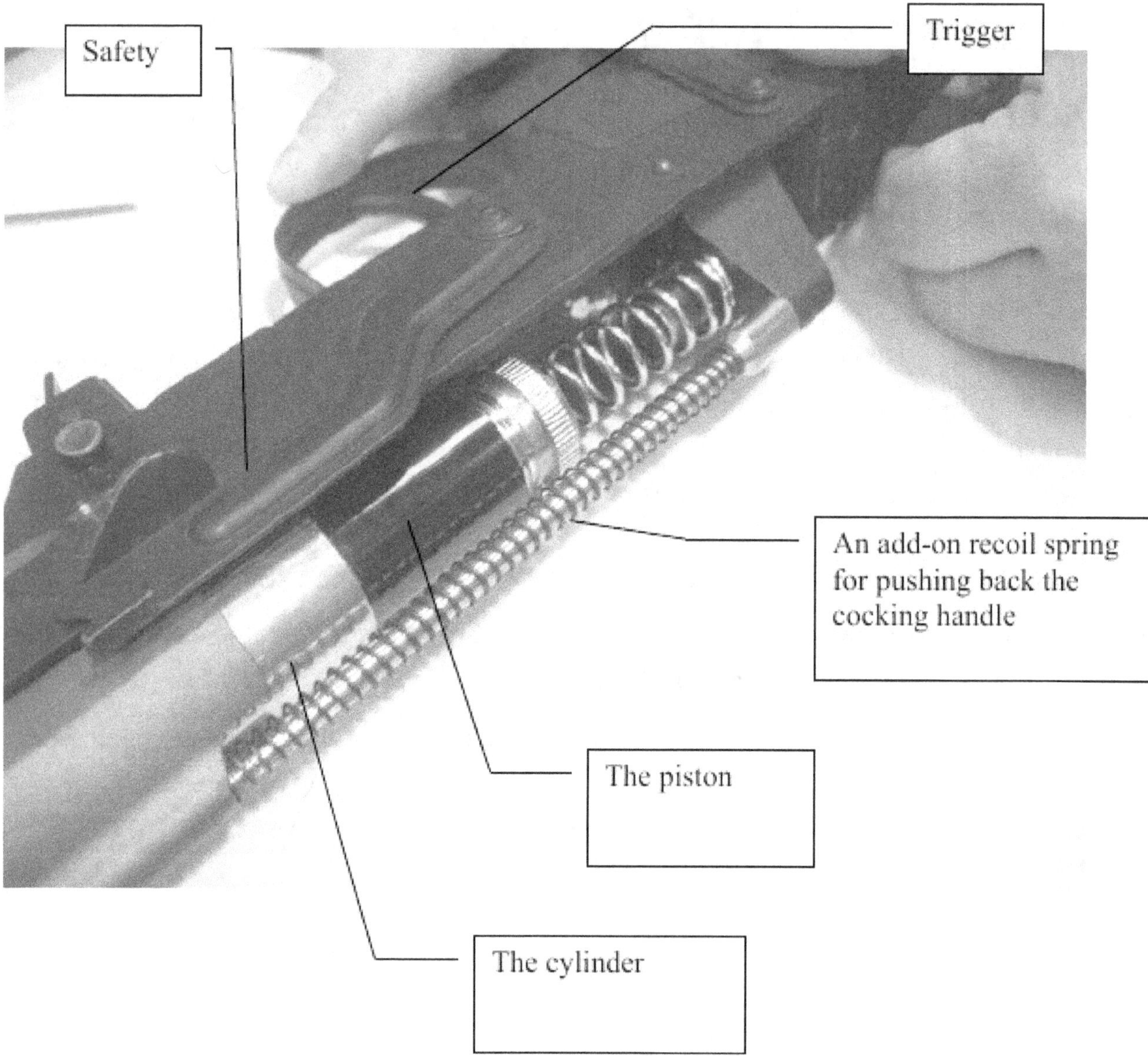

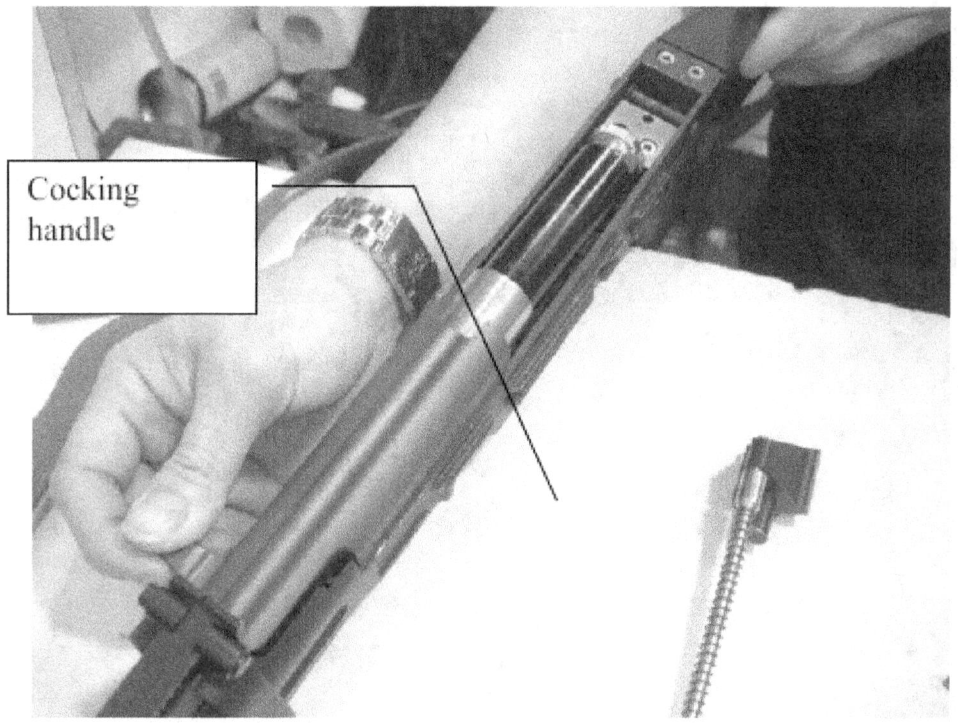

Cocking
handle

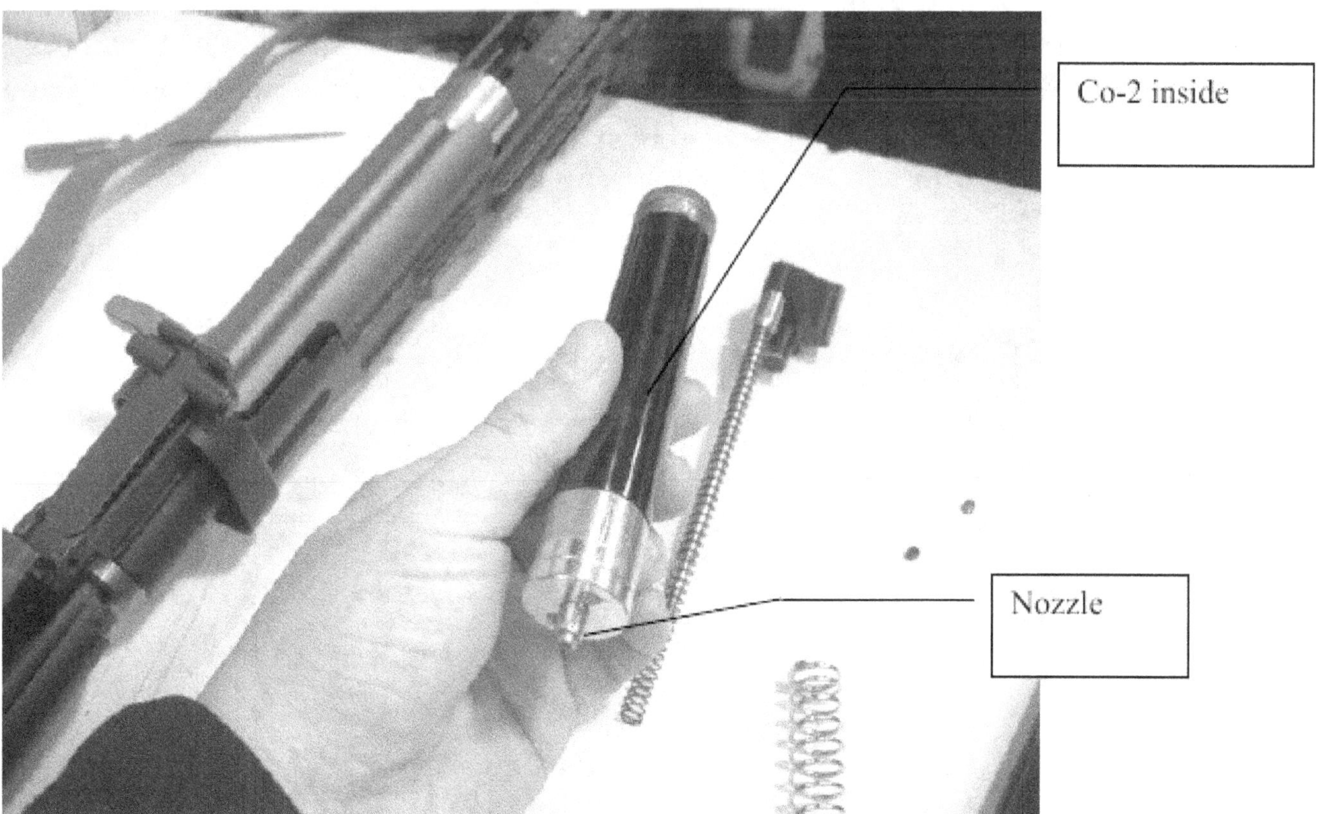

Co-2 inside
Nozzle

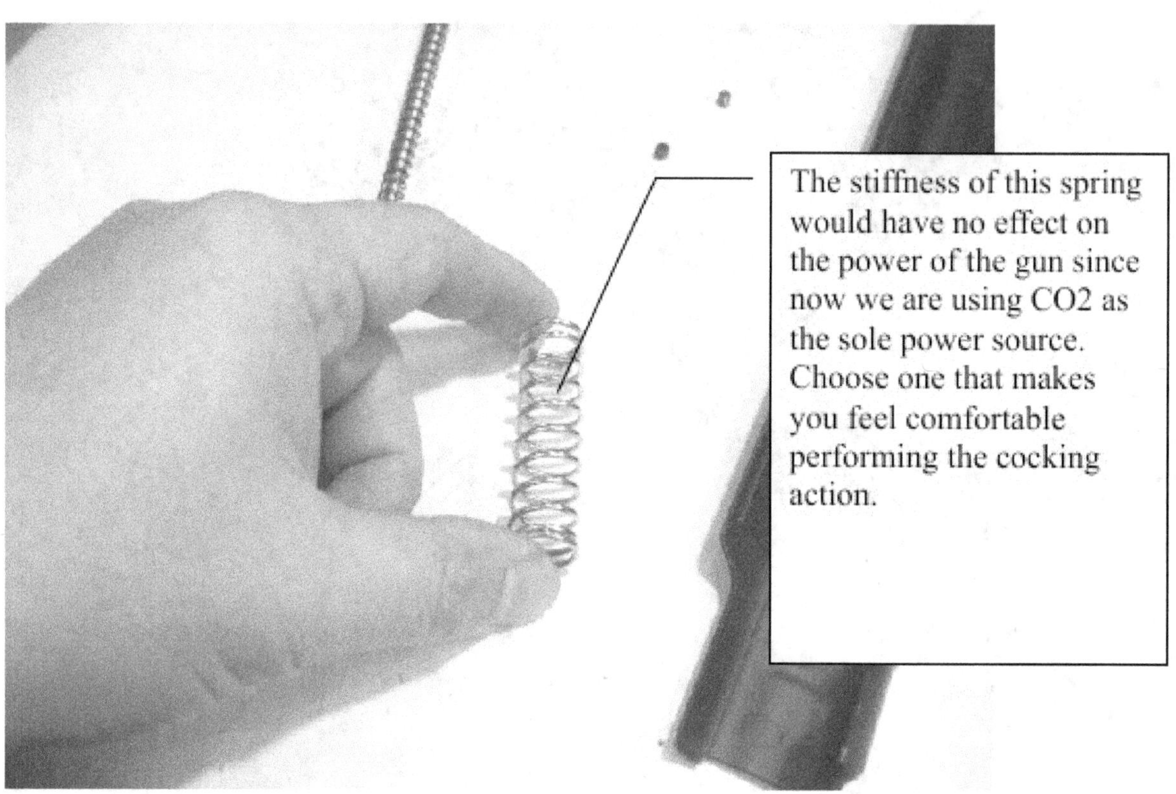

The original full length power spring is replaced by this much shorter recoil spring. This spring is placed behind the CO-2 piston. The original spring guide is also replaced with a shorter one.

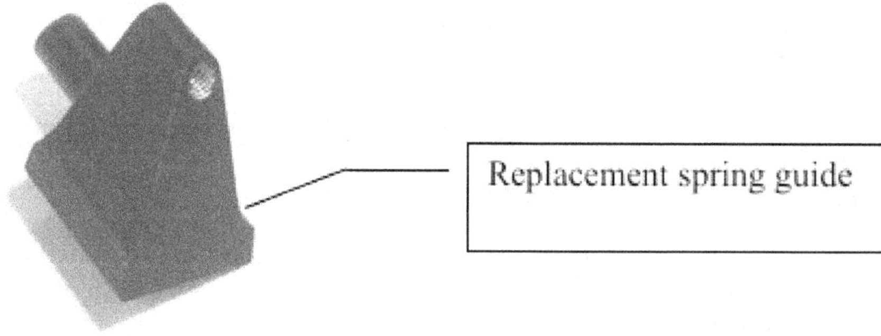

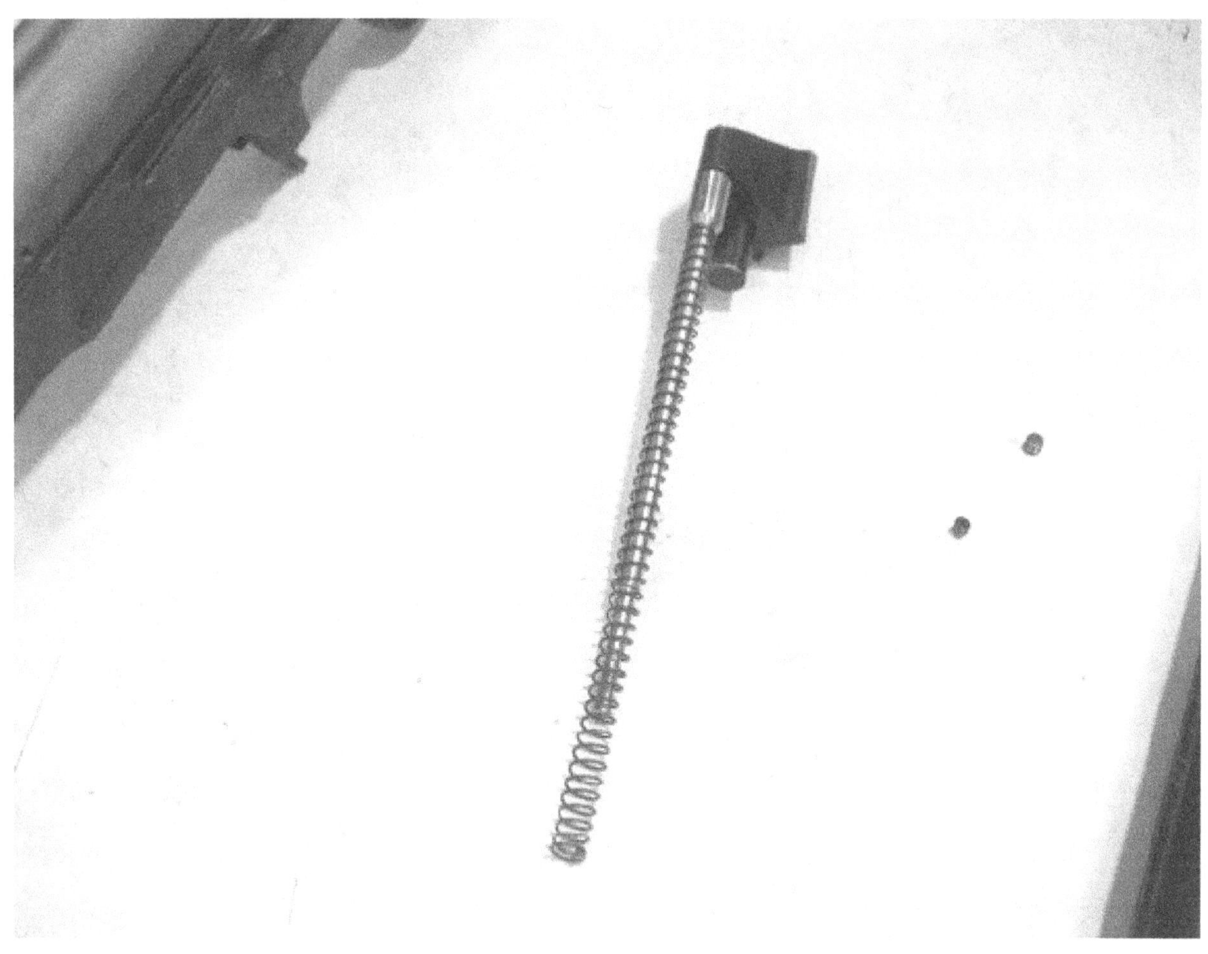

The recoil spring and the metal rod were manually crafted and mounted into the spring guide unit. Without this, after cocking you will have to manually push back the handle to the starting position. It has NOTHING TO DO WITH BLOWBACK. In fact, this CO2 upgrade provides no blowback function.

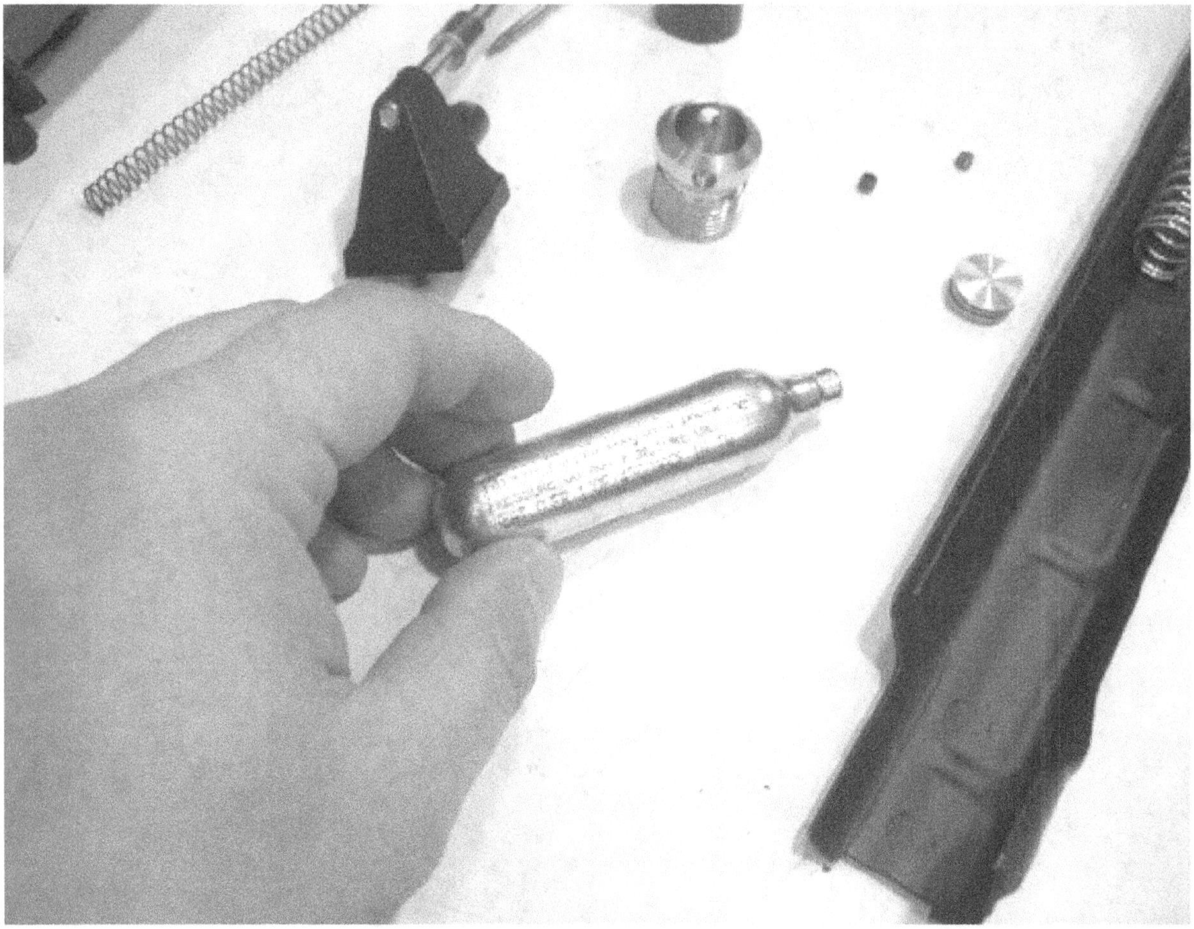

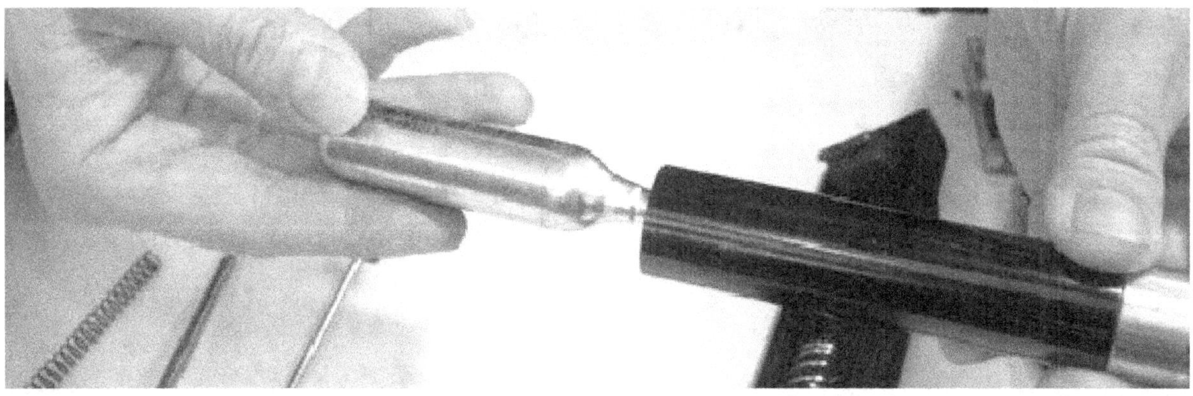

The piston can hold one CO2 cartridge. The cartridge is "unsealed" the moment you tighten up the piston.

CO2 is pretty sensitive to heat, therefore the cartridges must be stored at an appropriate temperature, below 120 degrees Fahrenheit or 49 degrees Celsius, although preferably even less.

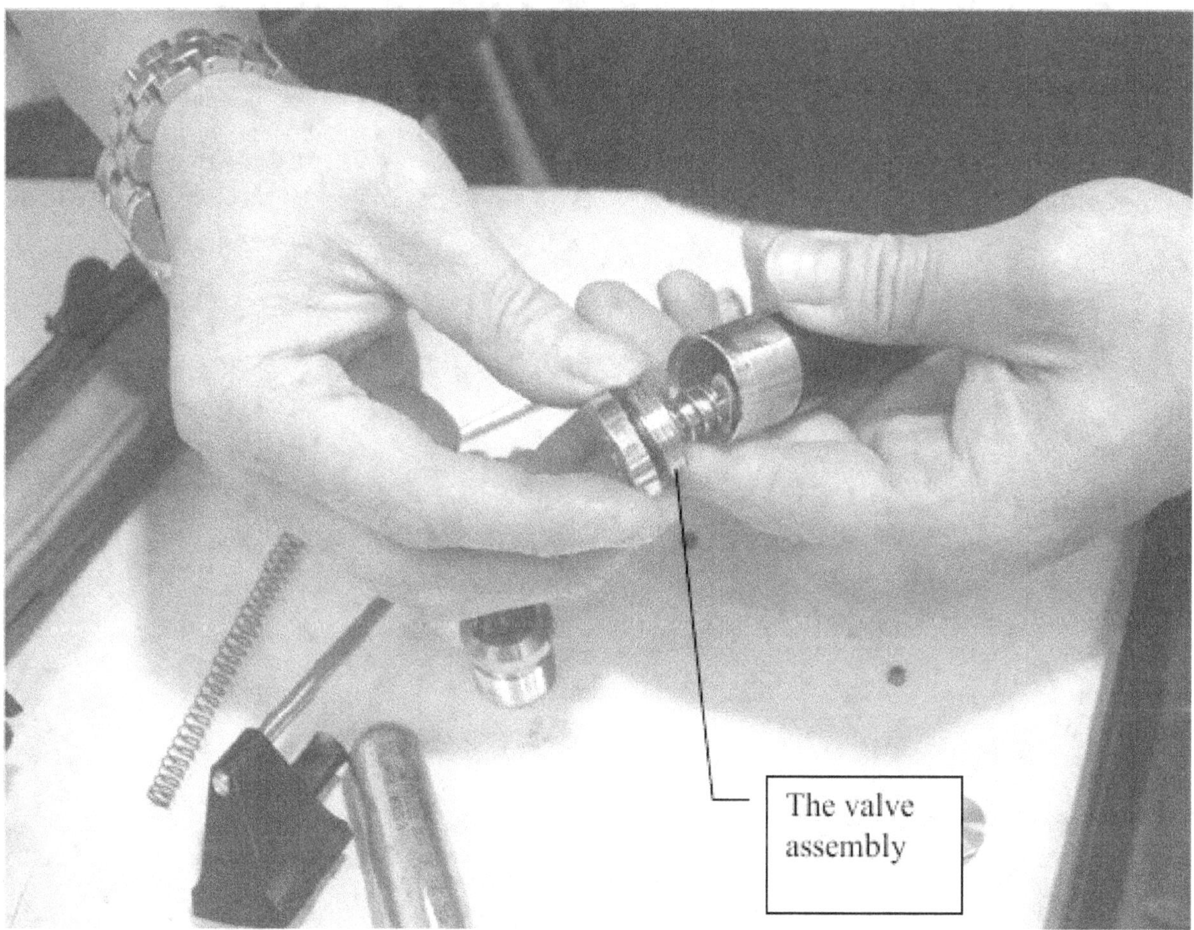

A valve is a device that can be used to control the flow of gases. Also known as regulators, valves can be found in everywhere in the architecture of a gas gun. There are a number of different designs for valves, depending on how they are being used in the gun. Valves can also vary from the extremely basic to the extraordinarily complex.

The gas is injected into the reservoir inside the piston. By pulling the trigger, the pressurized gas is released at the valve and channeled through a directed nozzle at the bullet, creating the pressure necessary to launch the bullet out of the barrel.

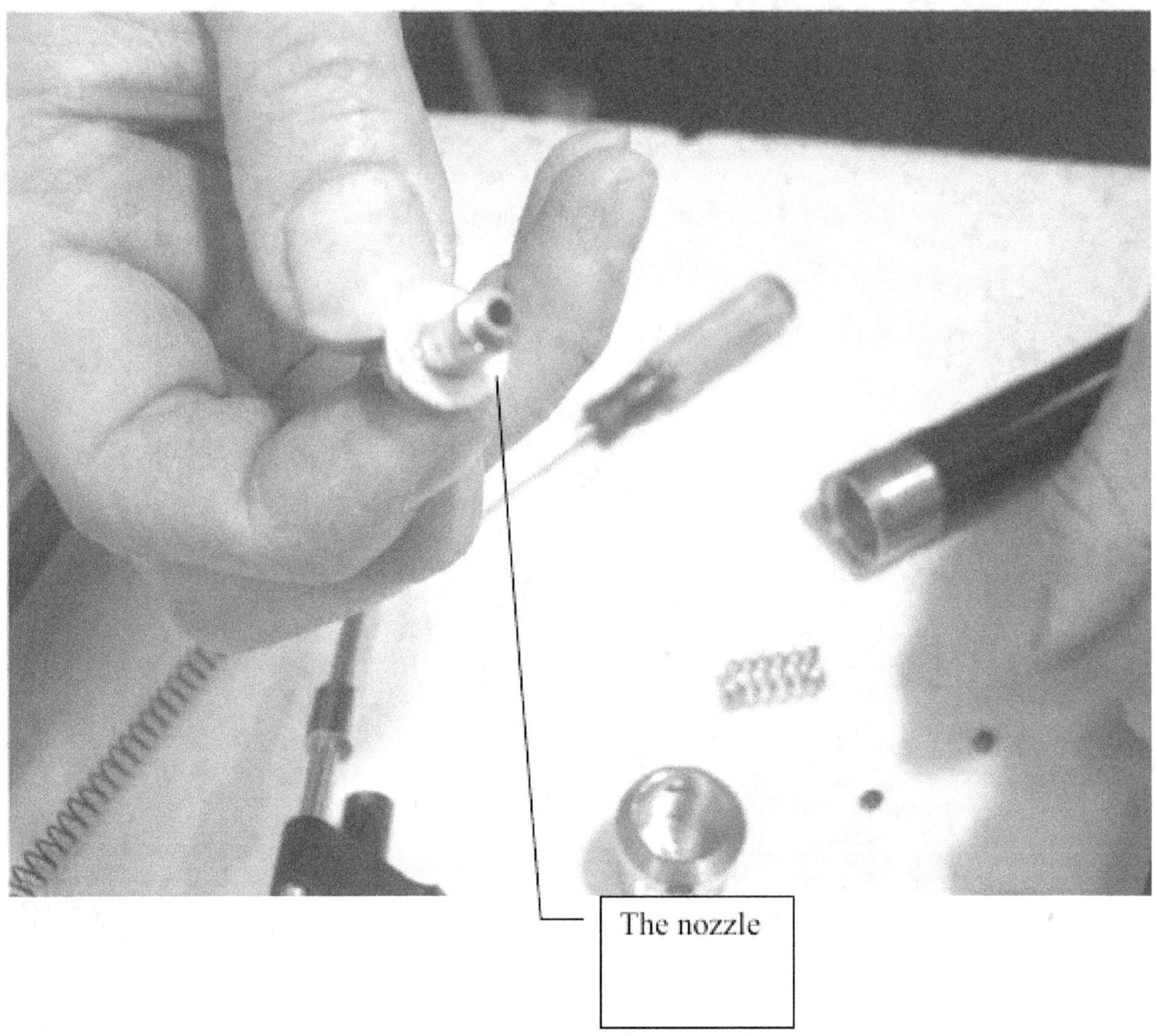

The kit is designed to allow for a quick swap. In other words, you can turn the springer into a CO2 powered gun very quickly.

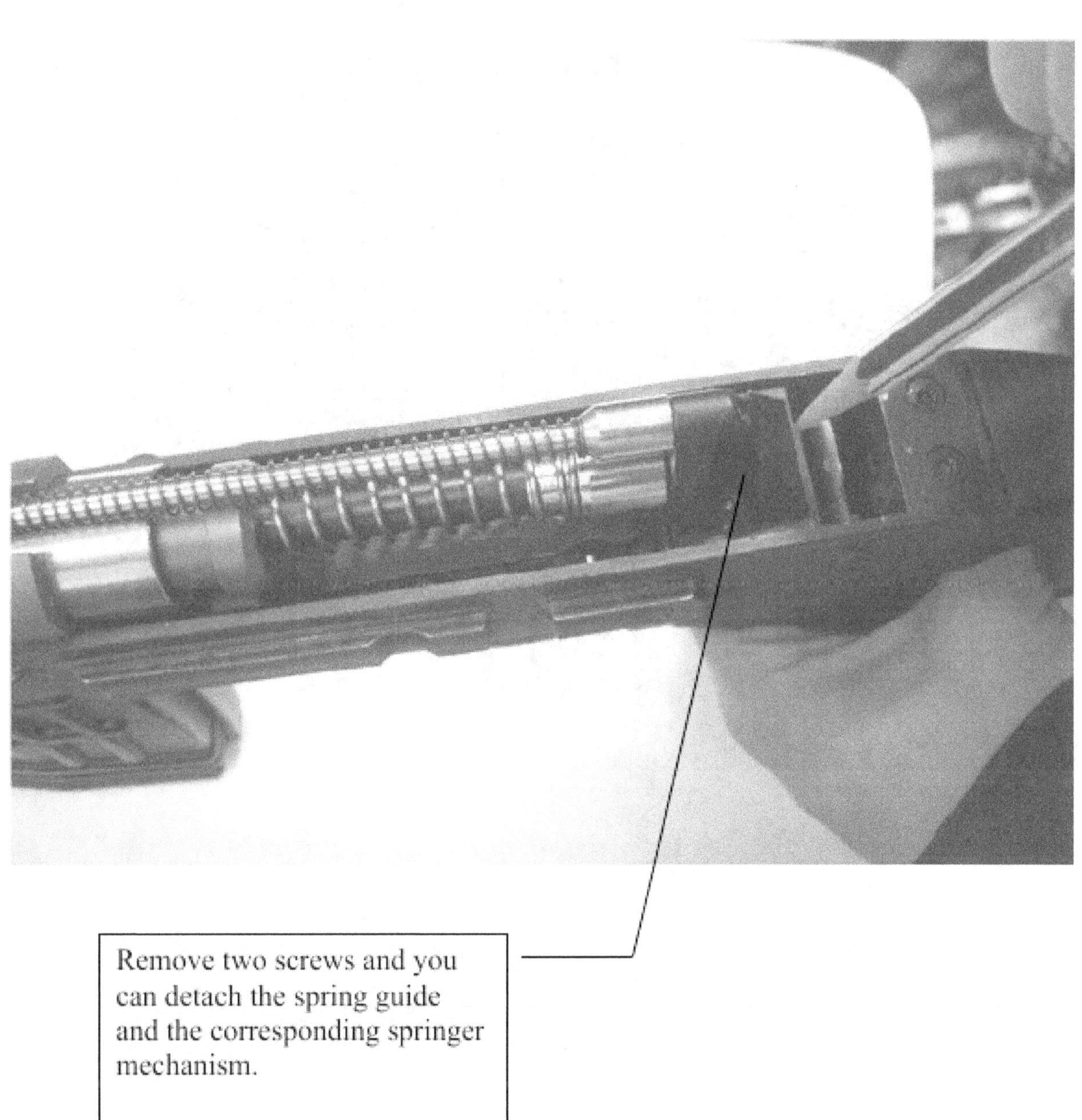

Remove two screws and you can detach the spring guide and the corresponding springer mechanism.

Hex screws

STRUCTURE OVERVIEW

The SVD Sniper with CO2 upgrade has the following major components:

- The front assembly, which includes the inner barrel, the outer barrel and the barrel supporting structure.

- The body, which includes the receiver and the upper cover.

- The grip and the butt stock as a one-piece component.

- The internals, which includes the cocking mechanism and the CO2 kit.

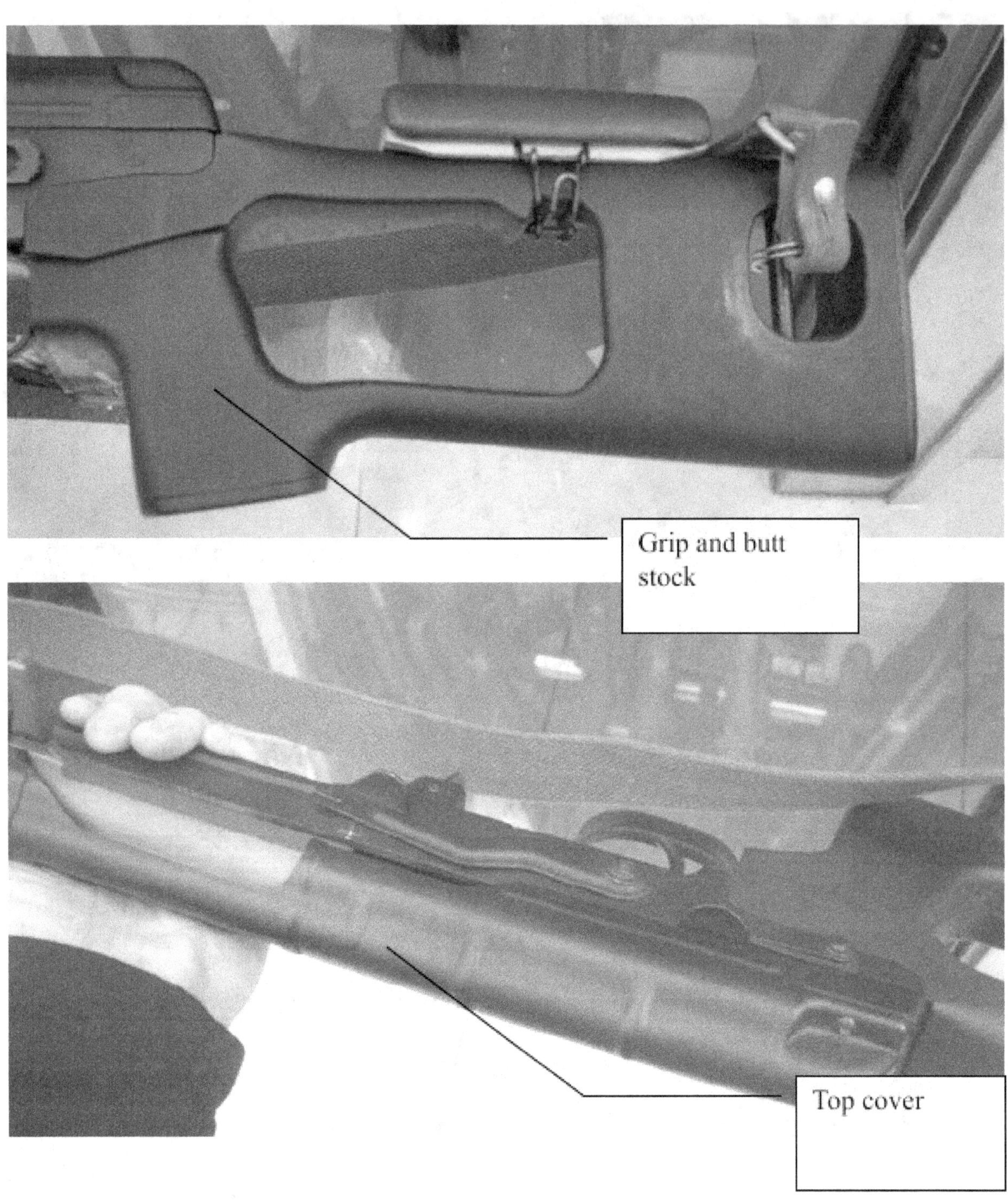

Grip and butt stock
Top cover

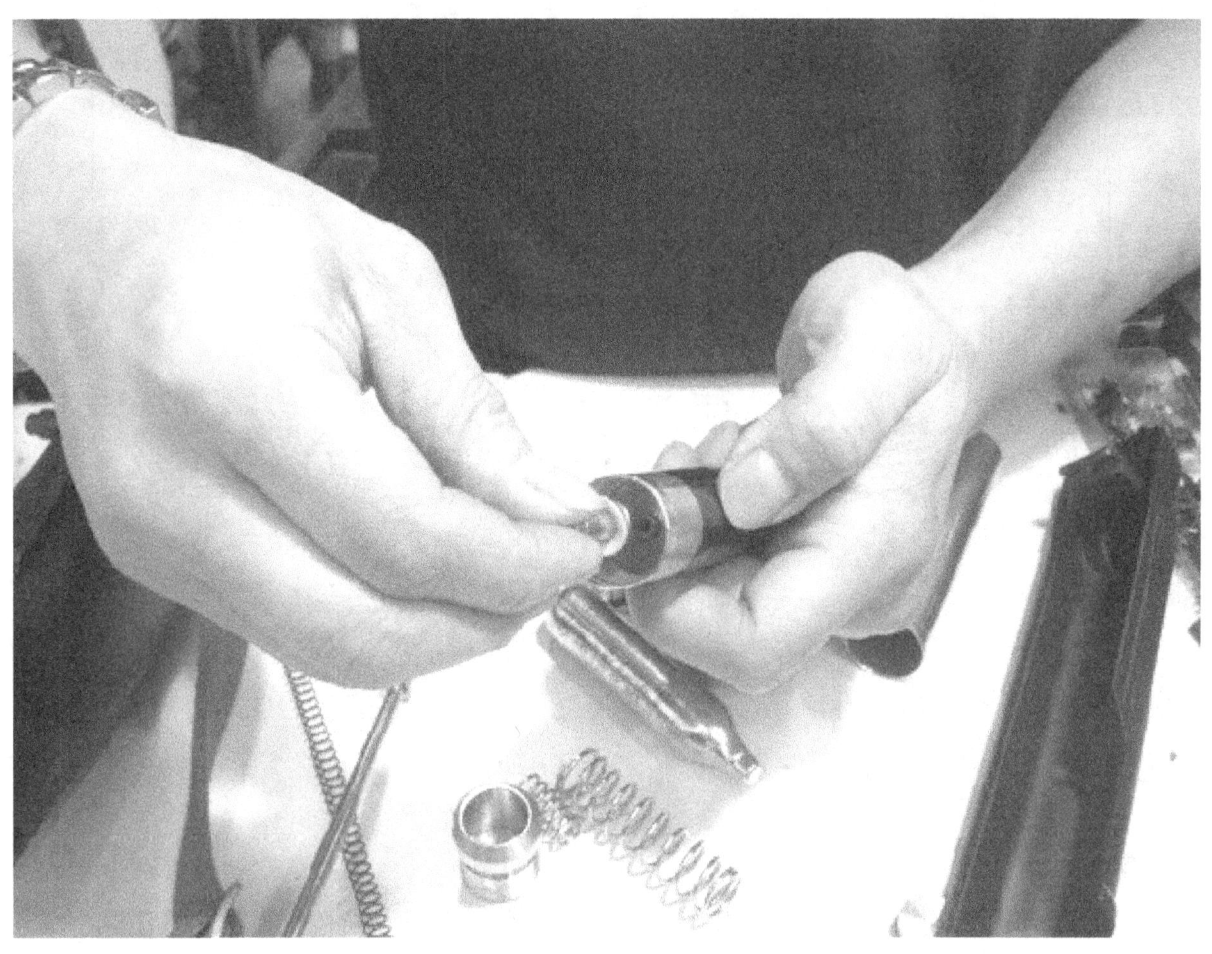

Why CO2? First you need to understand the difference between the various types of gas. The standard small can gas that comes with most Japanese/Taiwanese gas guns are 134a. 134a offers gentle power which is good enough for low impact application (mostly below 260fps). It offers relatively lower pressure than the so-called "green gas" and "red gas". Due to the low pressure nature, the rubber rings and valves of the gas system are less likely to break. However, it may not be powerful enough to serve a sniper gun.

* HFC-152a is a variation slightly more powerful than the 134a but is still considered to be too gentle for high FPS application.

"Green Gas" is "green" probably because it is said to be more environmental friendly. In fact, in some Asian countries the 134a is being referred to as green gas due to its environmental friendliness. Anyway, to avoid confusion, we prefer to use the names ET-1000, Top Gas and HFC 22 instead.

Top Gas is way more powerful than the 134a and is capable of delivering 280~360fps given proper gun design. Most Taiwanese gas guns have been reinforced to tolerate and take advantage of the high pressure provided by Top Gas. The problem is, the gas is not portable due to the lack of a cartridge format.

"Red Gas" is even more powerful than the Top Gas. It is "red" because the container can has a red color. This gas offers very high pressure and is NOT suitable for most off-the-shelf gas guns. It is all about gas pressure. Those more powerful gases offer very high pressure which could be unsustainable by the stock valves and the rubber rings. In fact, on gas systems that are configured with "weaker" valves and rings, high power gases can blow things up in seconds.

CO2 is very powerful (even more powerful than Top Gas). Although it requires a special cylinder/piston combo to house the cartridge, it is highly portable and exchangeable. In fact, the cartridge has a size very easy to fit into the rifle.

An effective sniper gun must be powerful enough to achieve a practical range. CO2 is therefore an ideal choice.

Because there has to be room to house the CO2 cartridge, the spring guide has to be shorter than original. The picture below shows a comparison:

THE BODY ASSEMBLY

This photo shows the front assembly and the barrel supporting structure:

The SVD has a very long but solid front structure.

The top cover can be removed through the switch on the side.

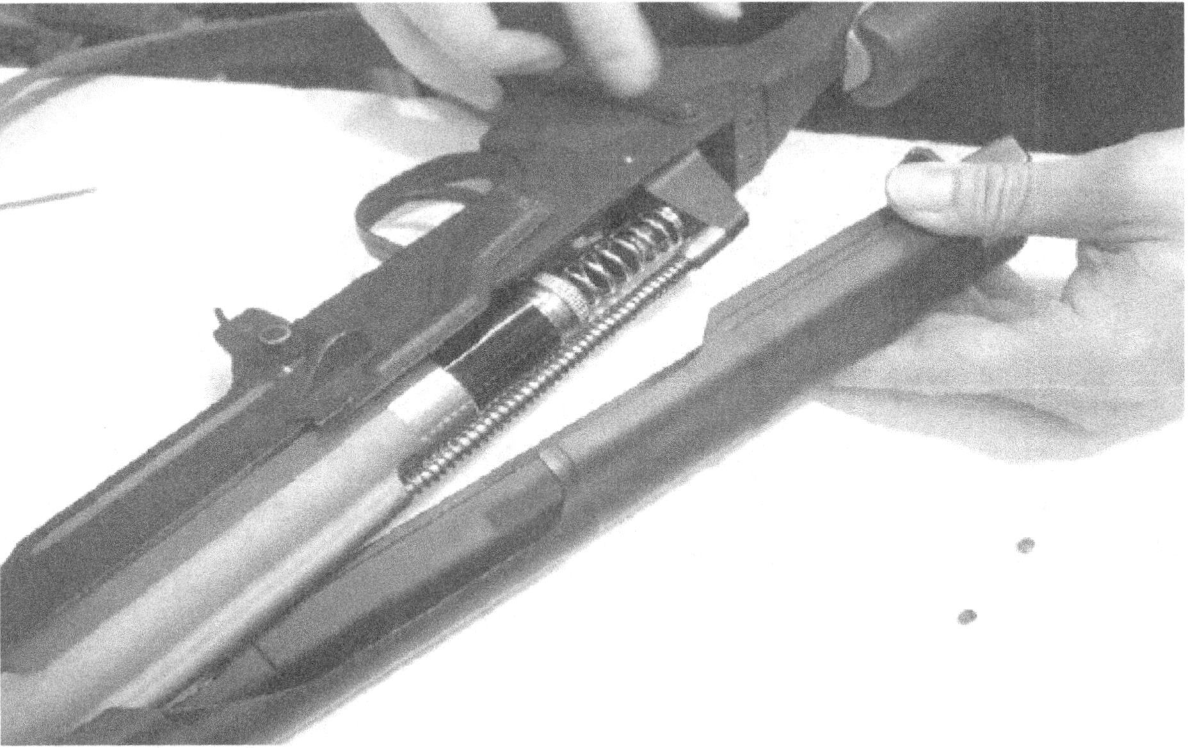

ACCESSING THE CO2 KIT

Whenever you want to expose the CO2 kit, you must first remove the top cover. This top cover is NOT AK compatible.

After removing the top cover, you can safely pull out the spring guide and the corresponding parts.

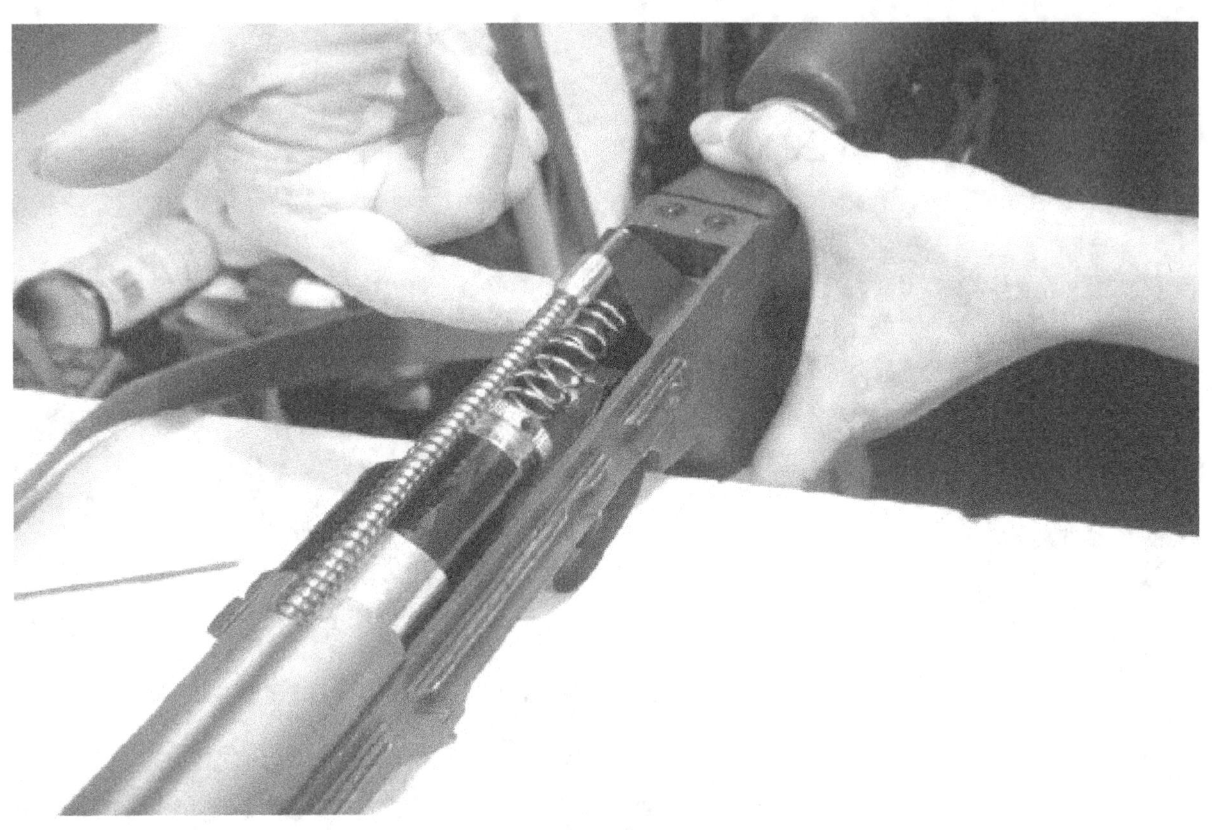

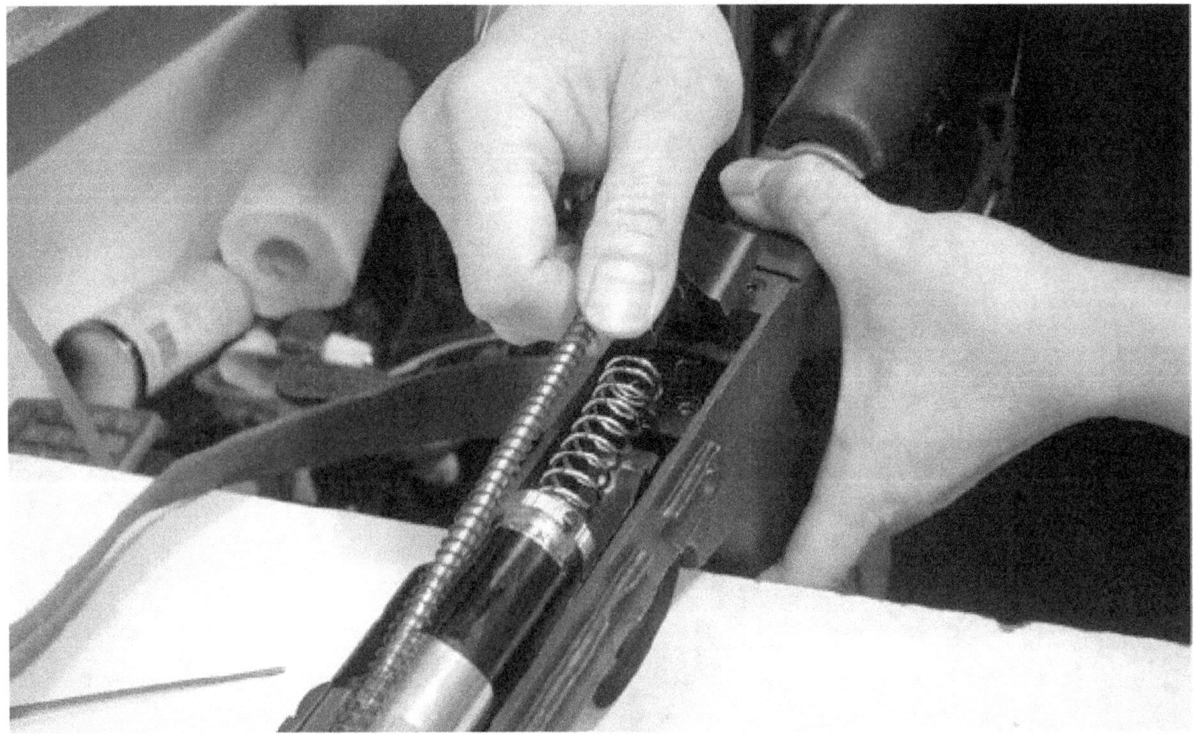

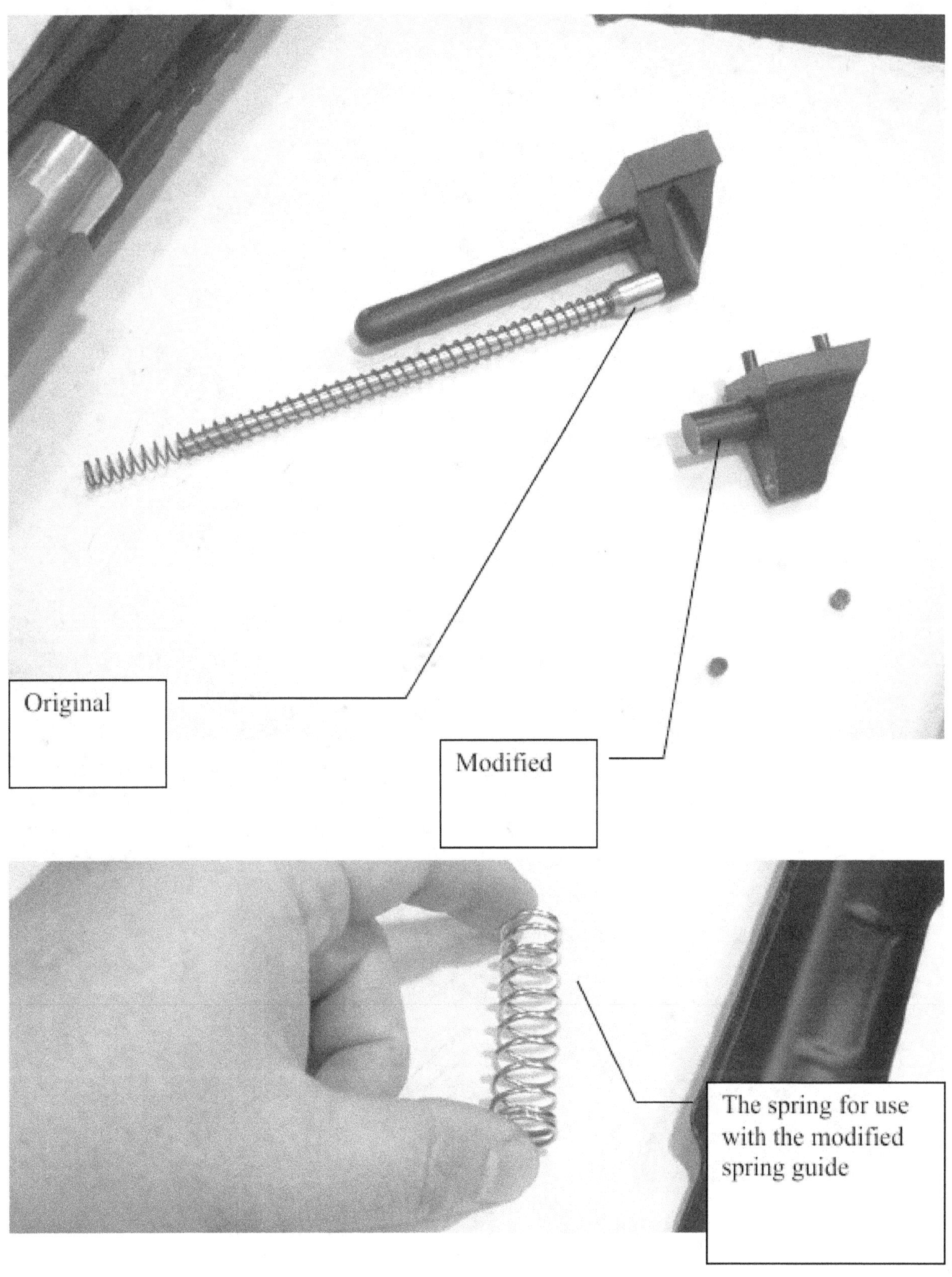

Original
Modified
The spring for use
with the modified
spring guide

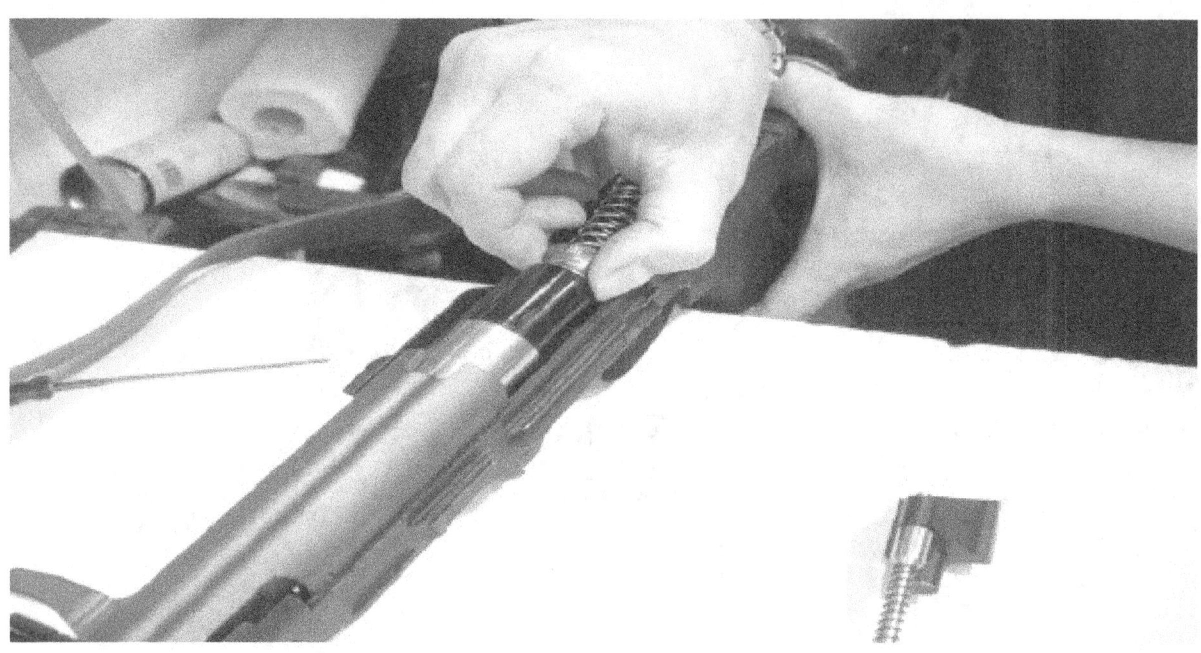

Now you can pull out the piston and then the cylinder set.

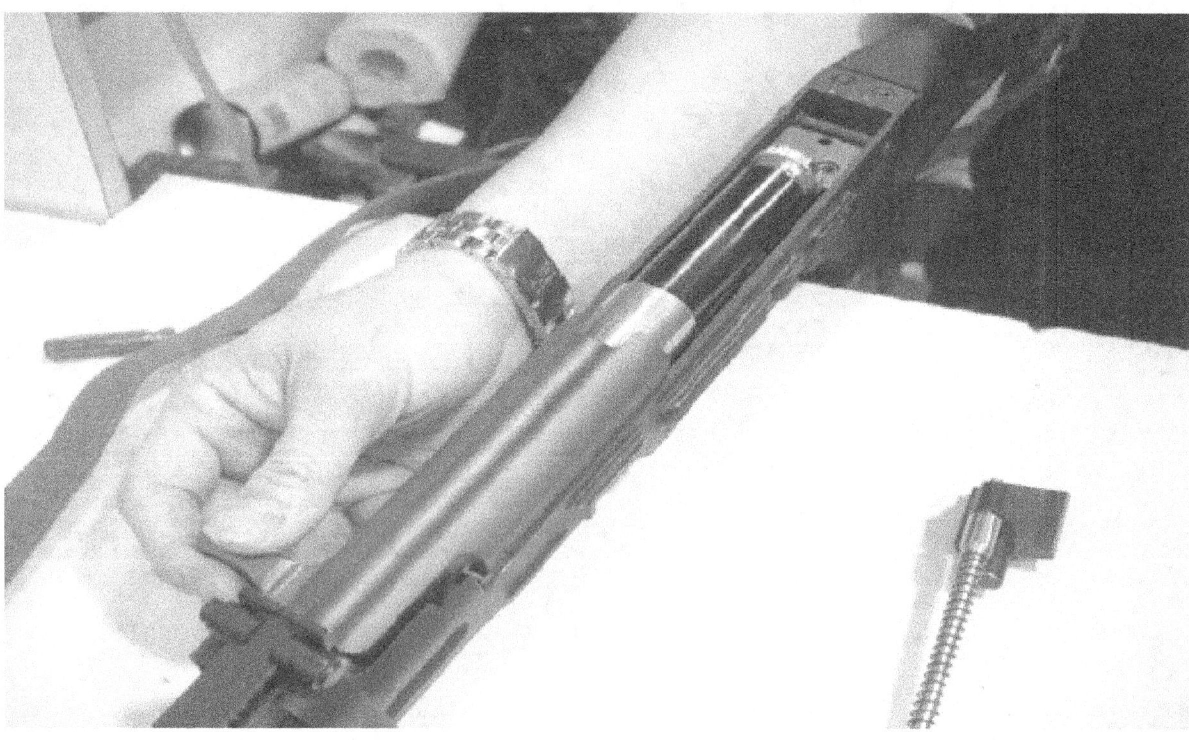

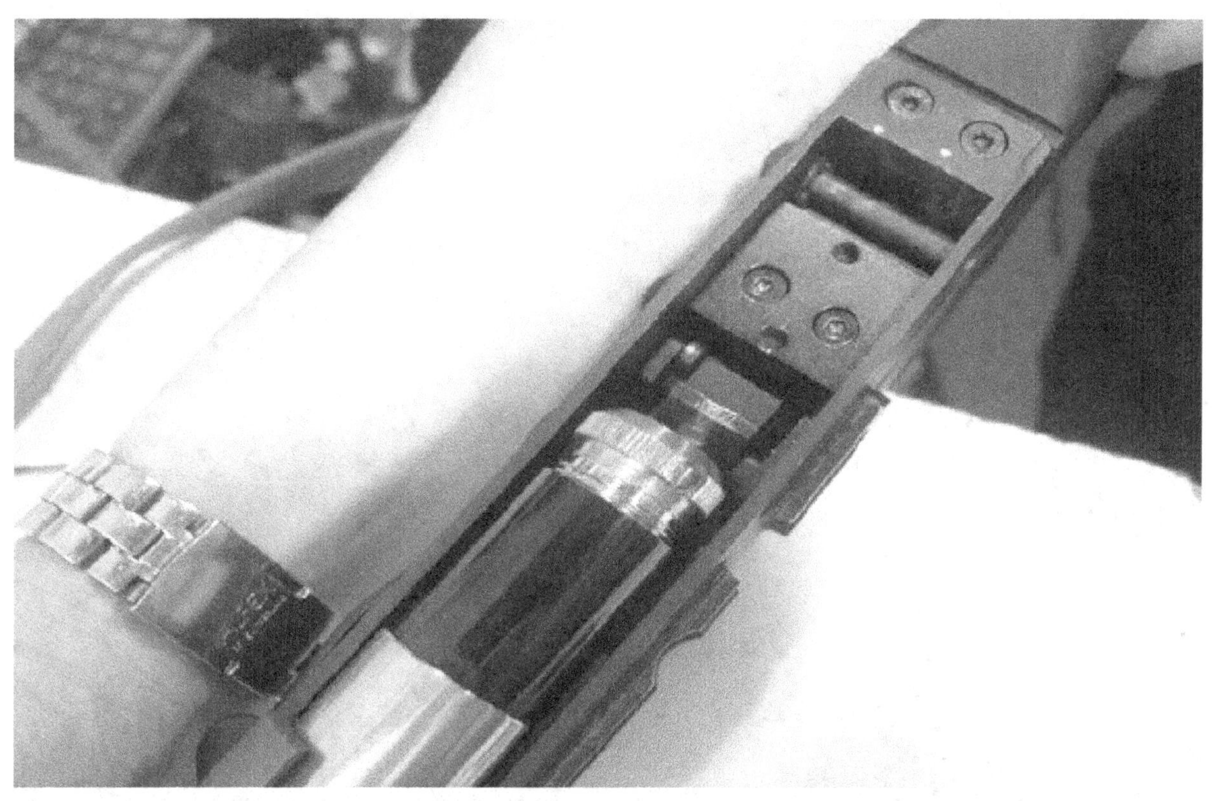

OPENING UP THE CO2 KIT

You need the help of a screw driver as a lever to open up the CO2 piston.

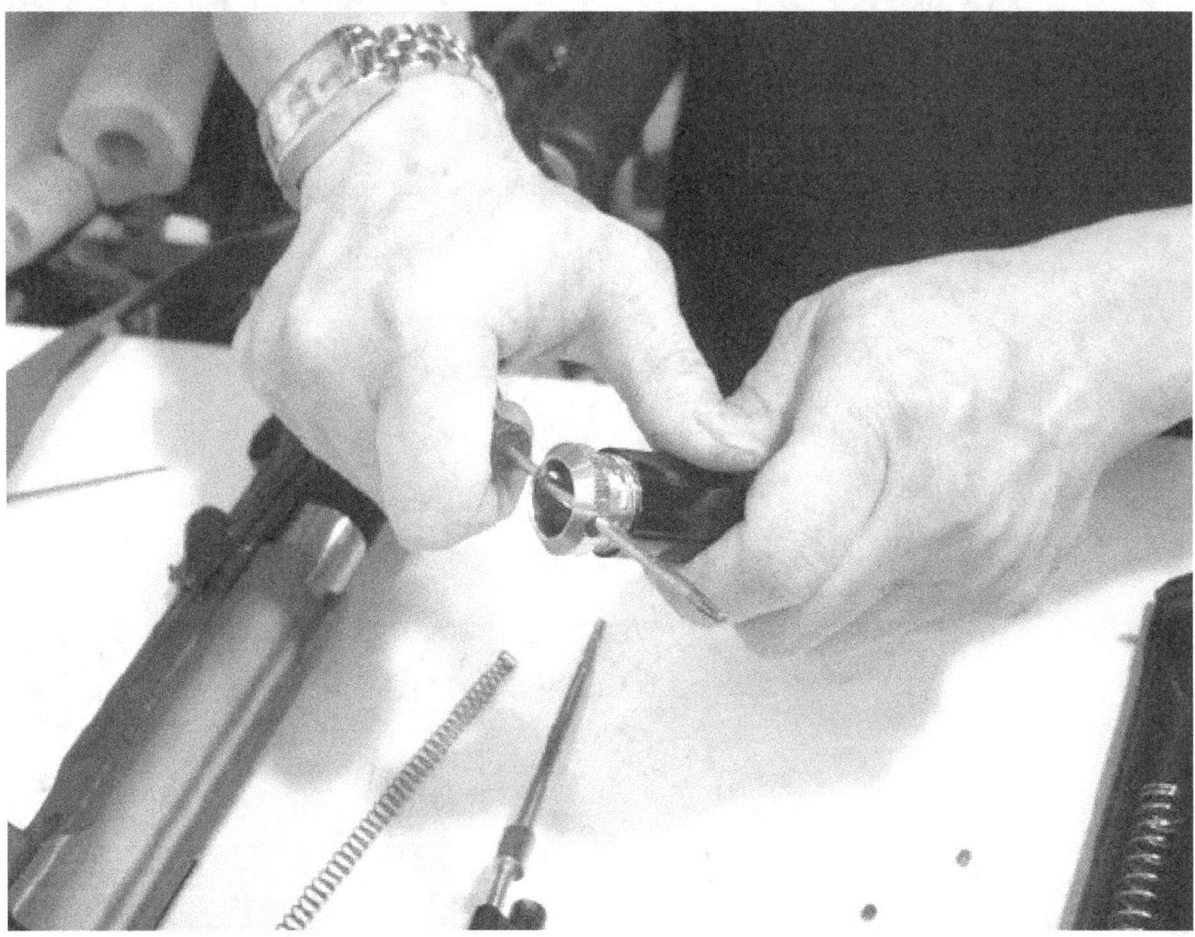

You want to know that once a cartridge is inserted into the piston and that the piston is closed tight, the cartridge seal is broken and you will not be able to reuse the cartridge somewhere else. With proper air seal, the gas will remain good inside the piston for a week or so.

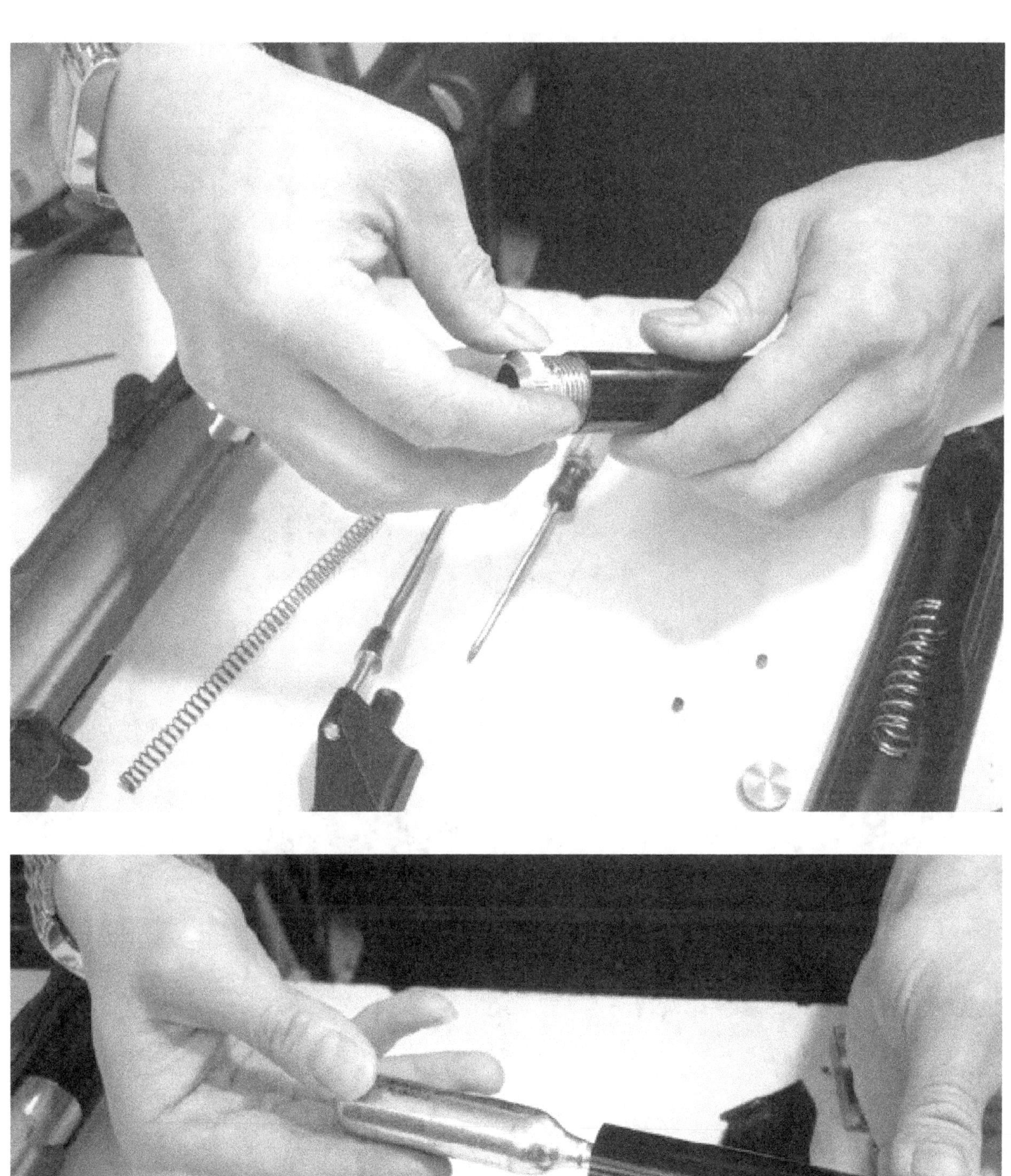

THE HEAD AND THE NOZZLE

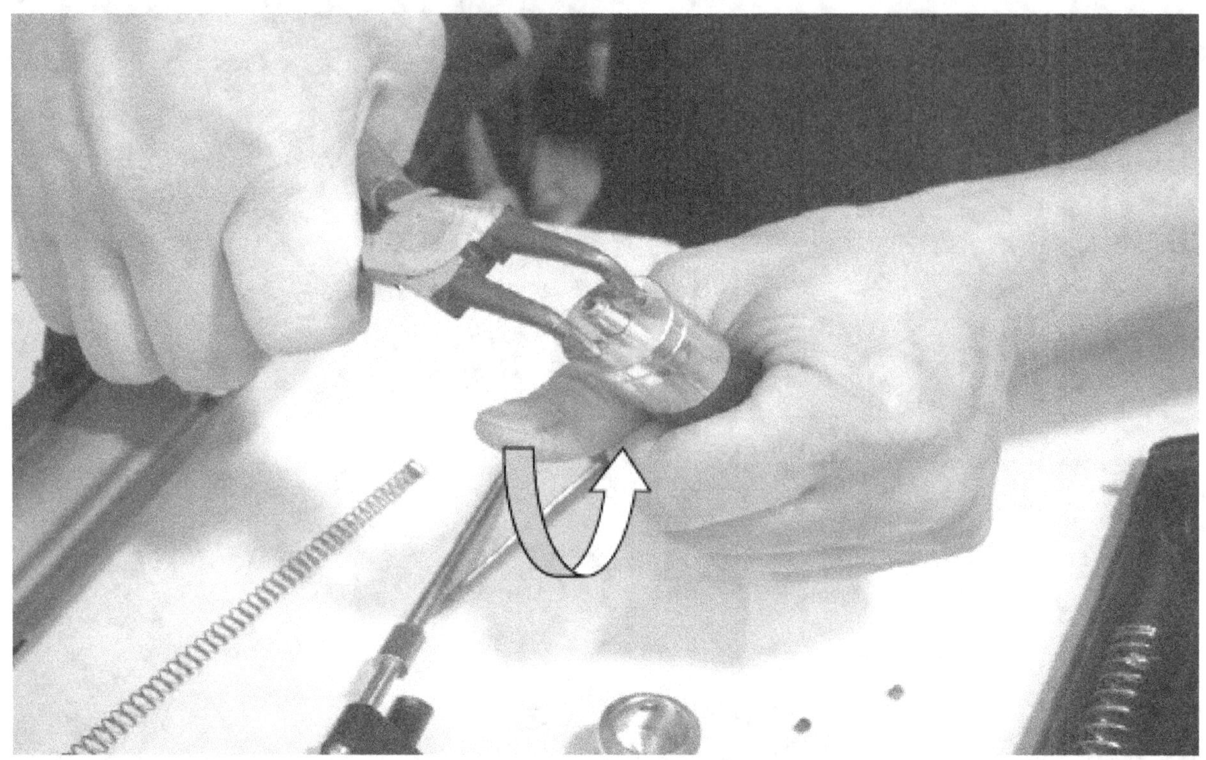

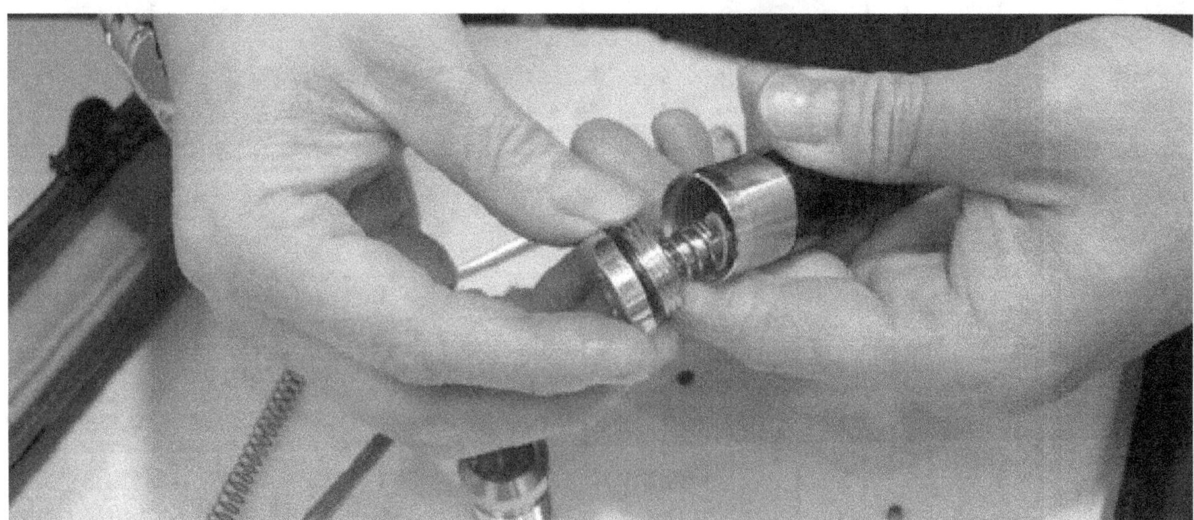

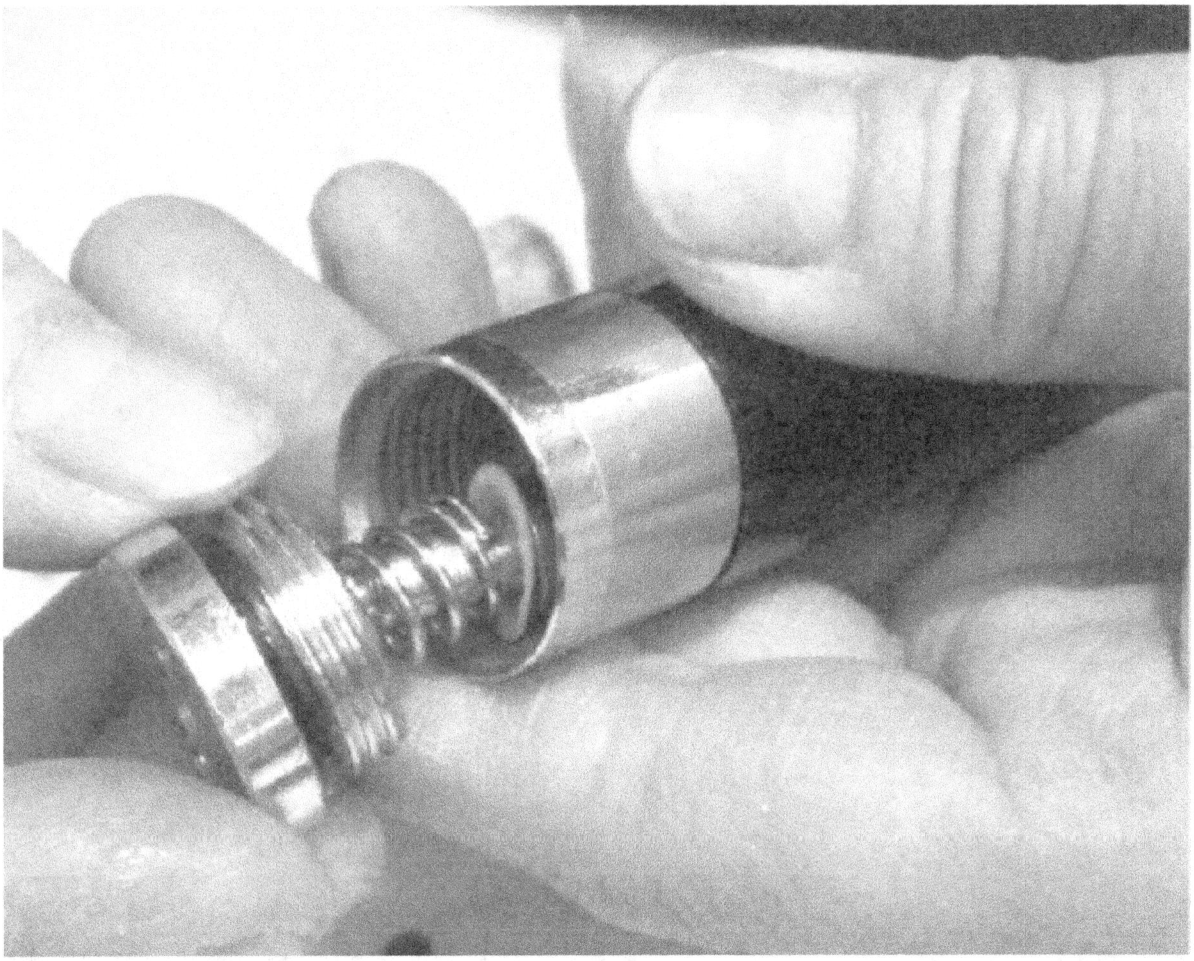

This O ring is the first defense against air leak. It may have to be replaced regularly.

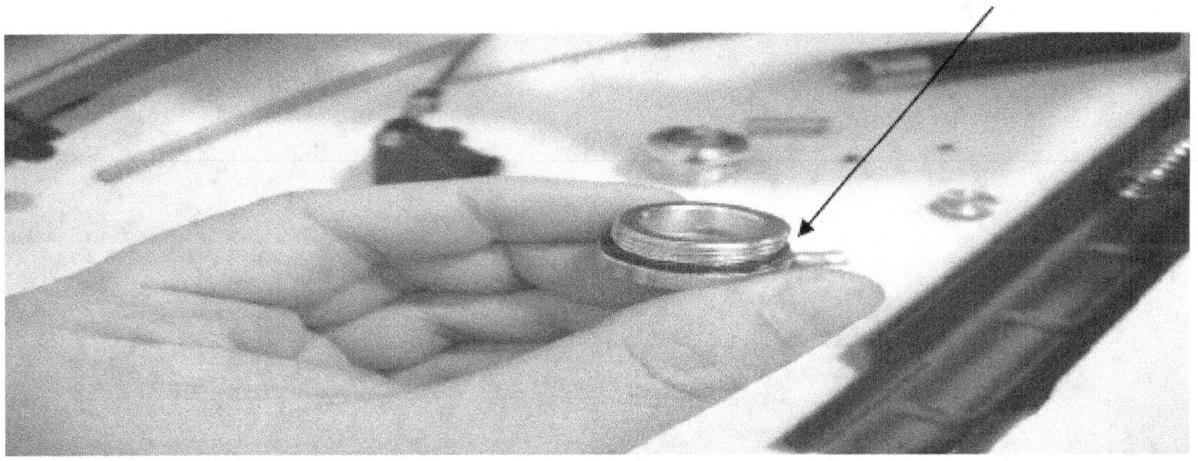

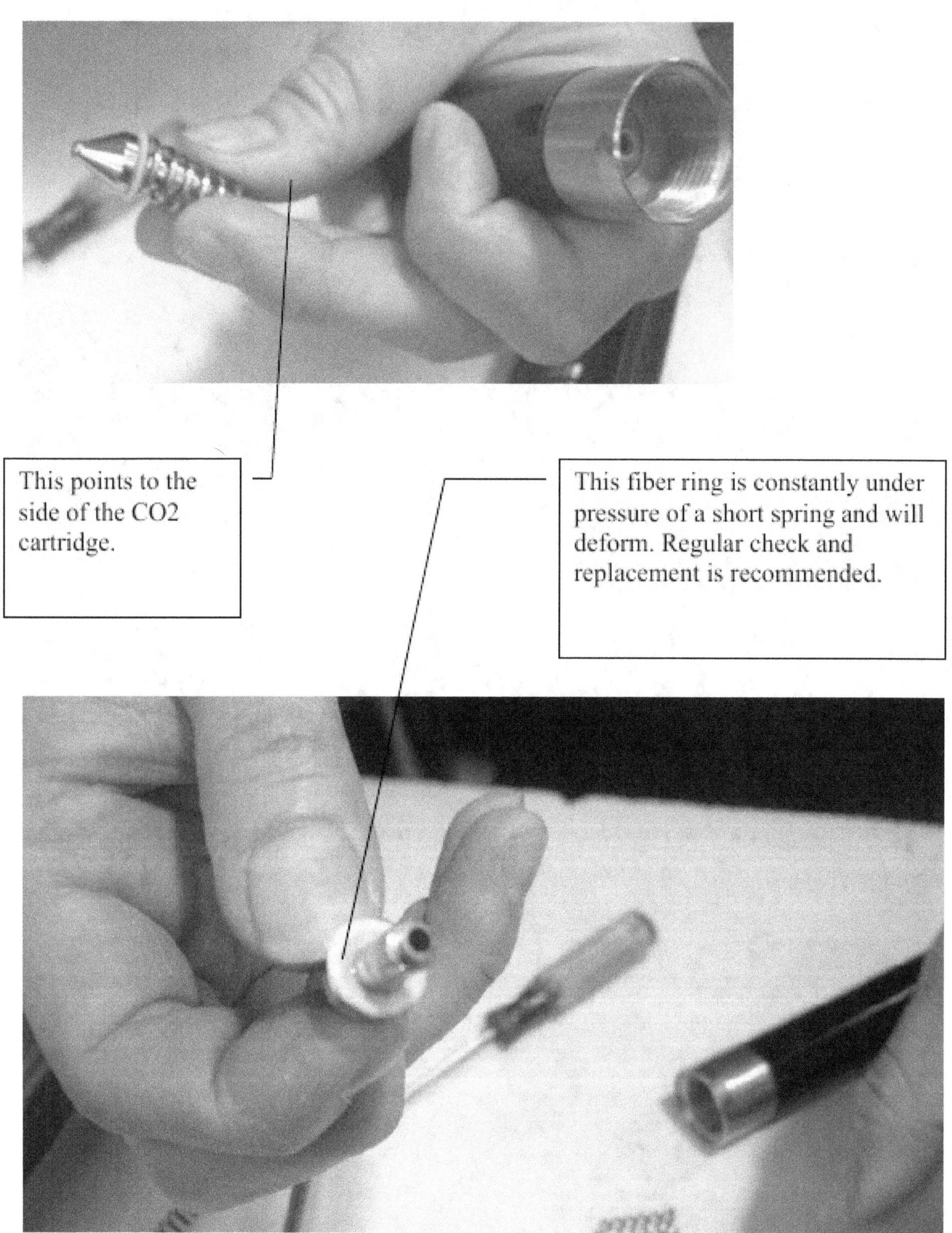

This points to the
side of the CO2
cartridge.

This fiber ring is constantly under
pressure of a short spring and will
deform. Regular check and
replacement is recommended.

THE CYLINDER HEAD

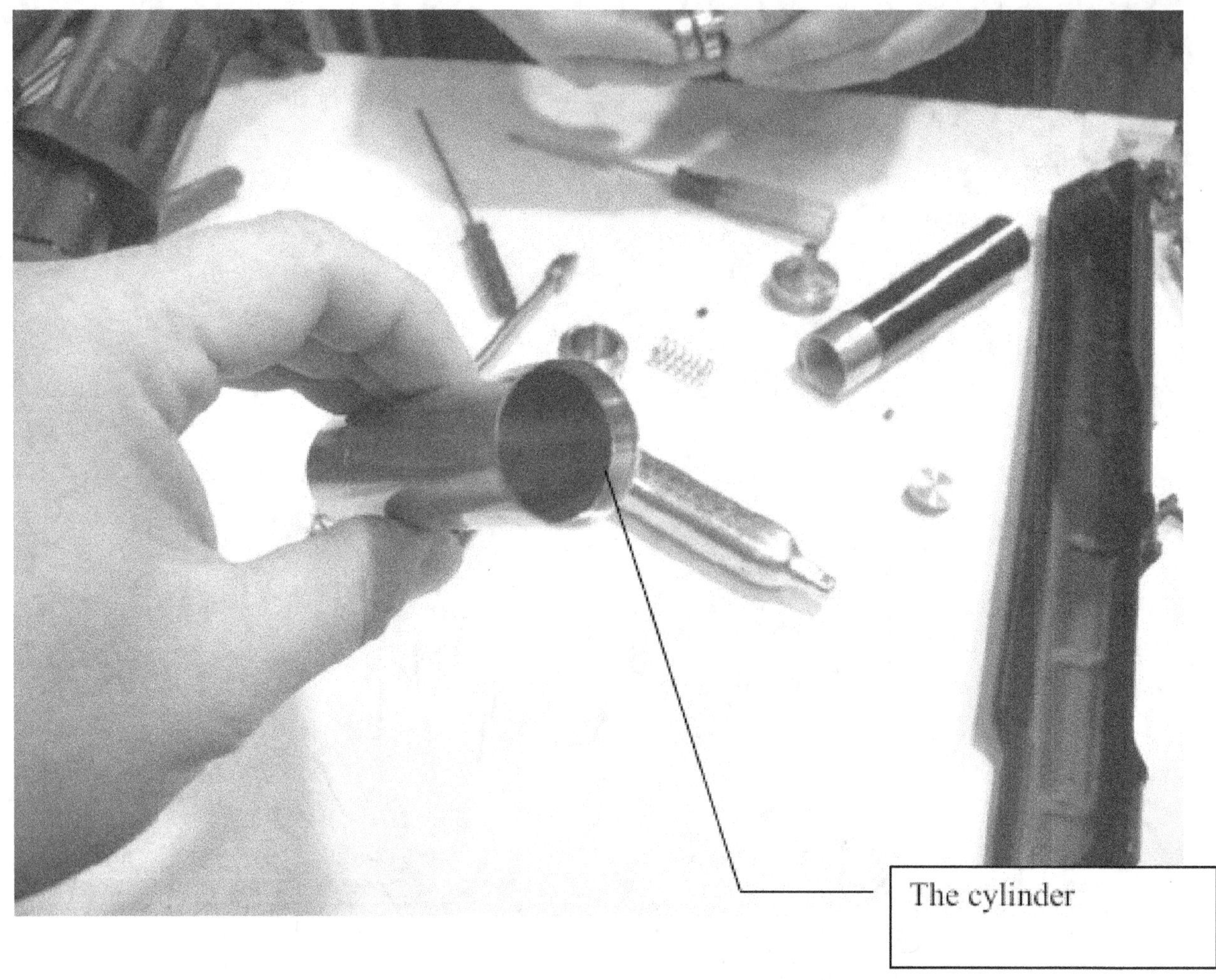

The cylinder and cylinder head "accommodate" the piston. The cylinder head has a rubber pad at the side facing the piston.

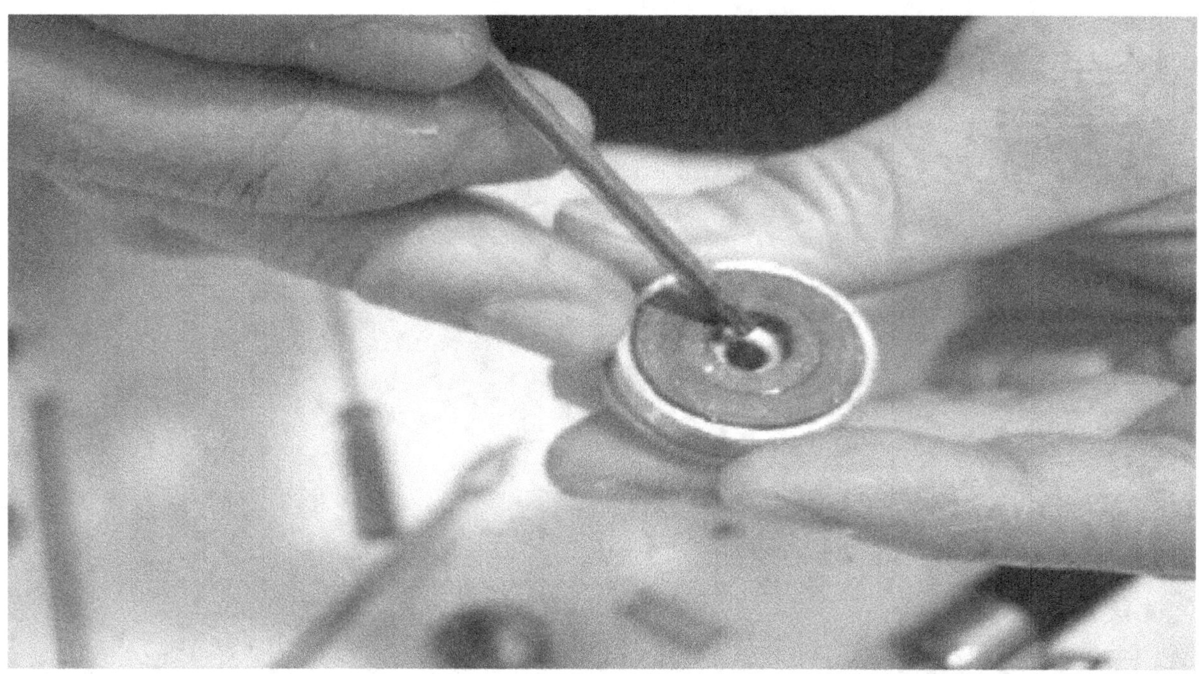

The cylinder head absorbs the impact of the piston. The nozzle of the piston passes through the cylinder opening so the gas can propel bullets.

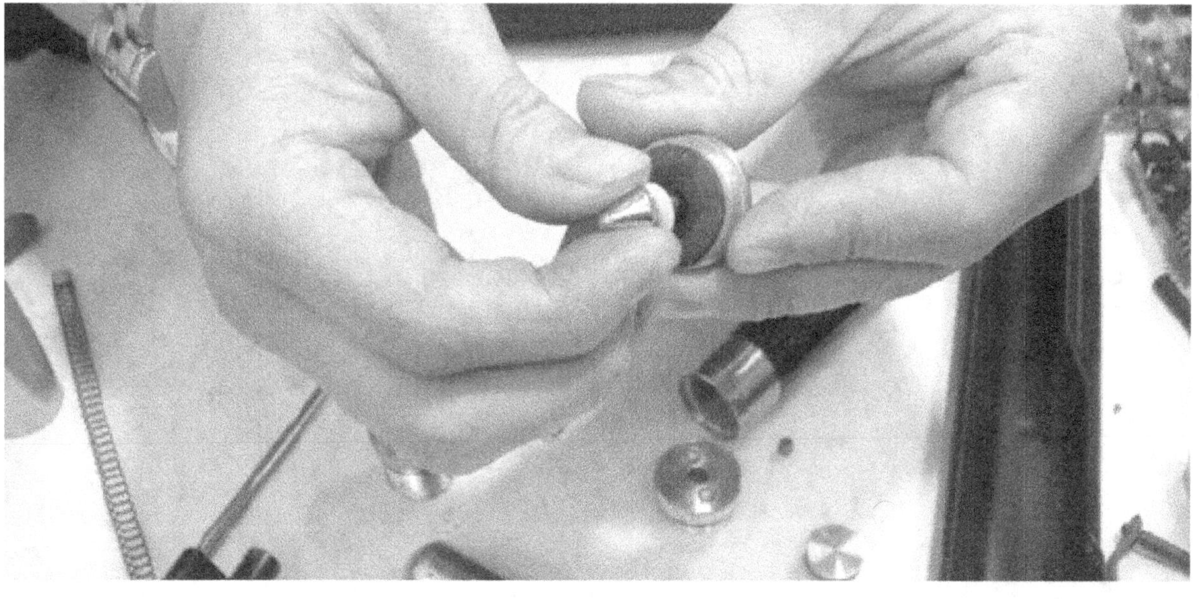

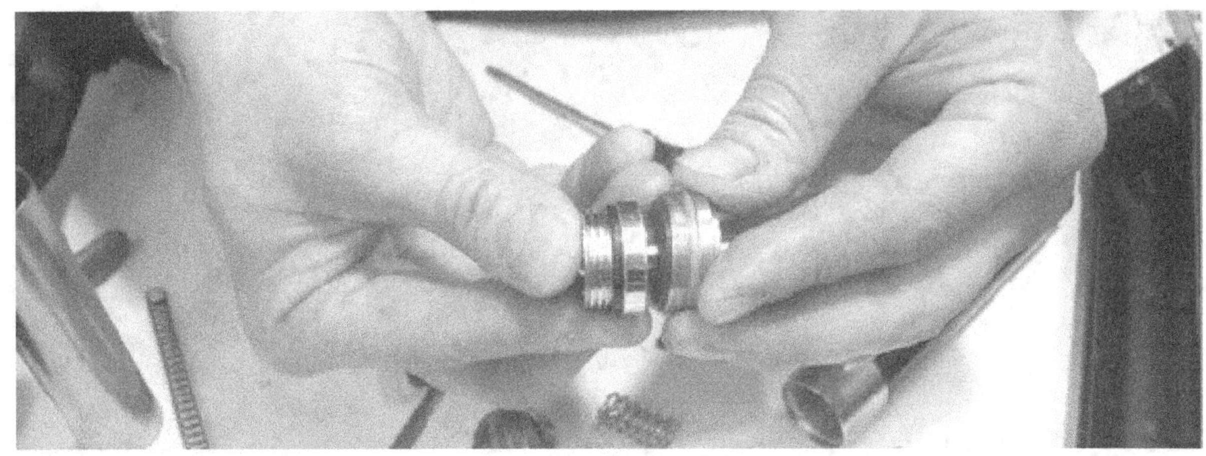

A perfect seal of the whole thing is critical to shooting power.

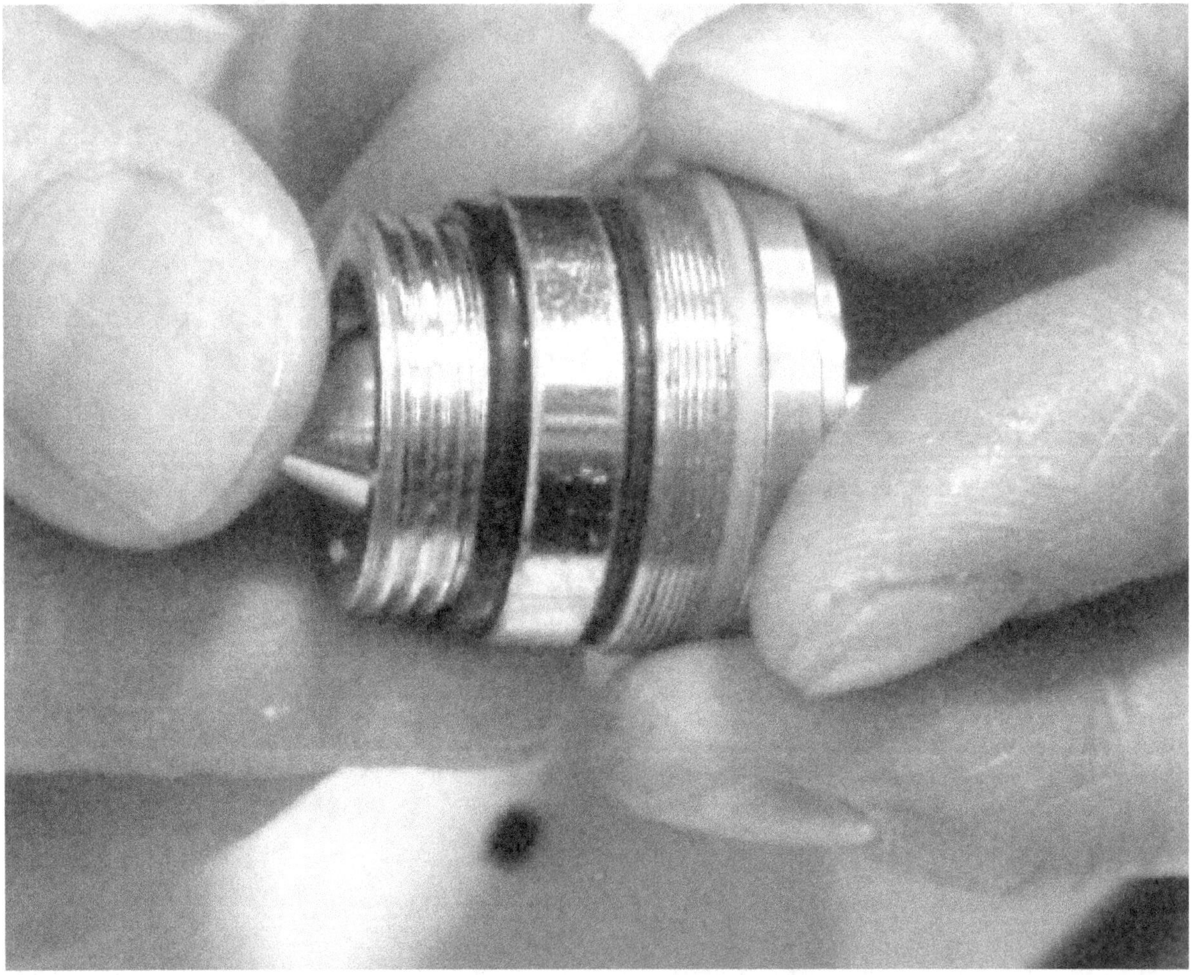

THE FRONT ASSEMBLY

To expose the barrel, first you loosen the front sight. There are several hex screws to remove.

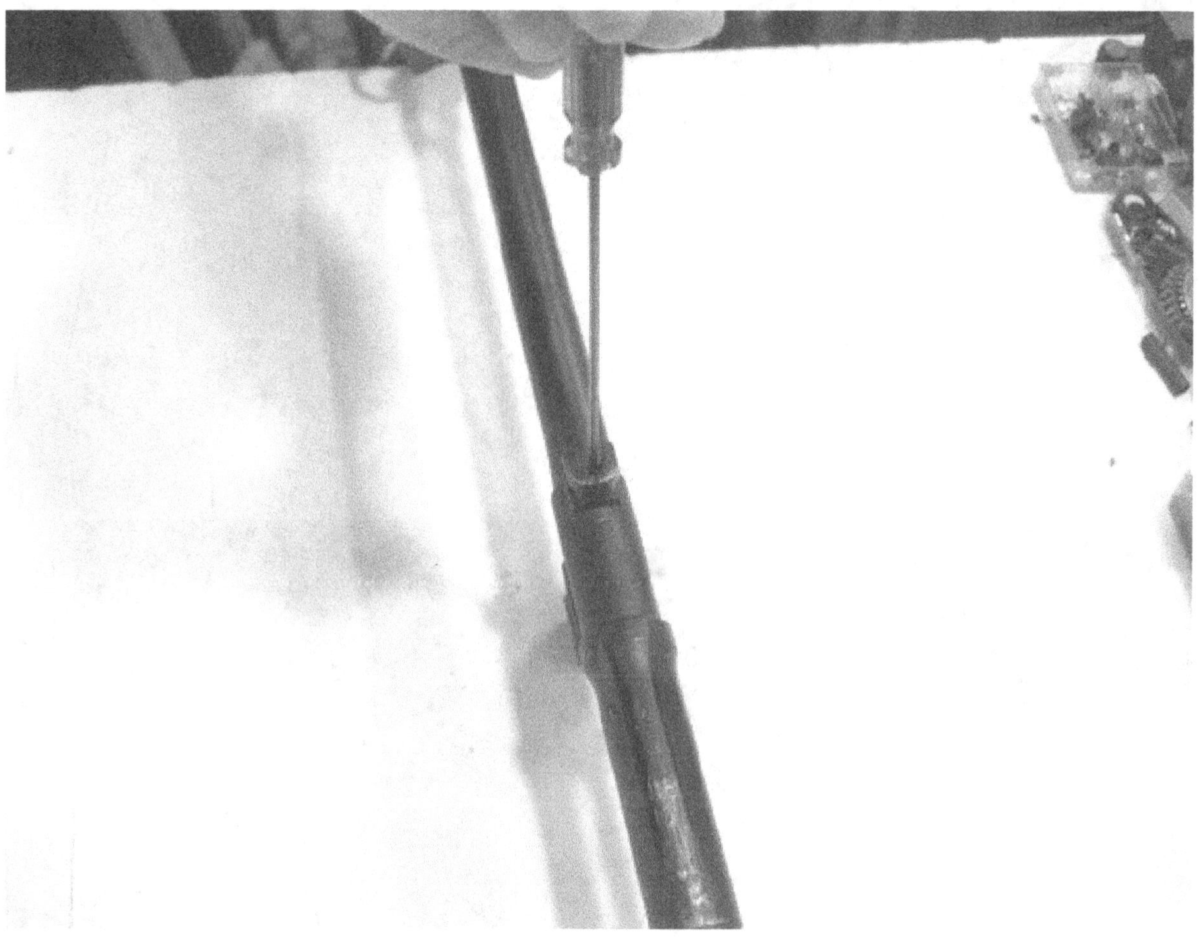

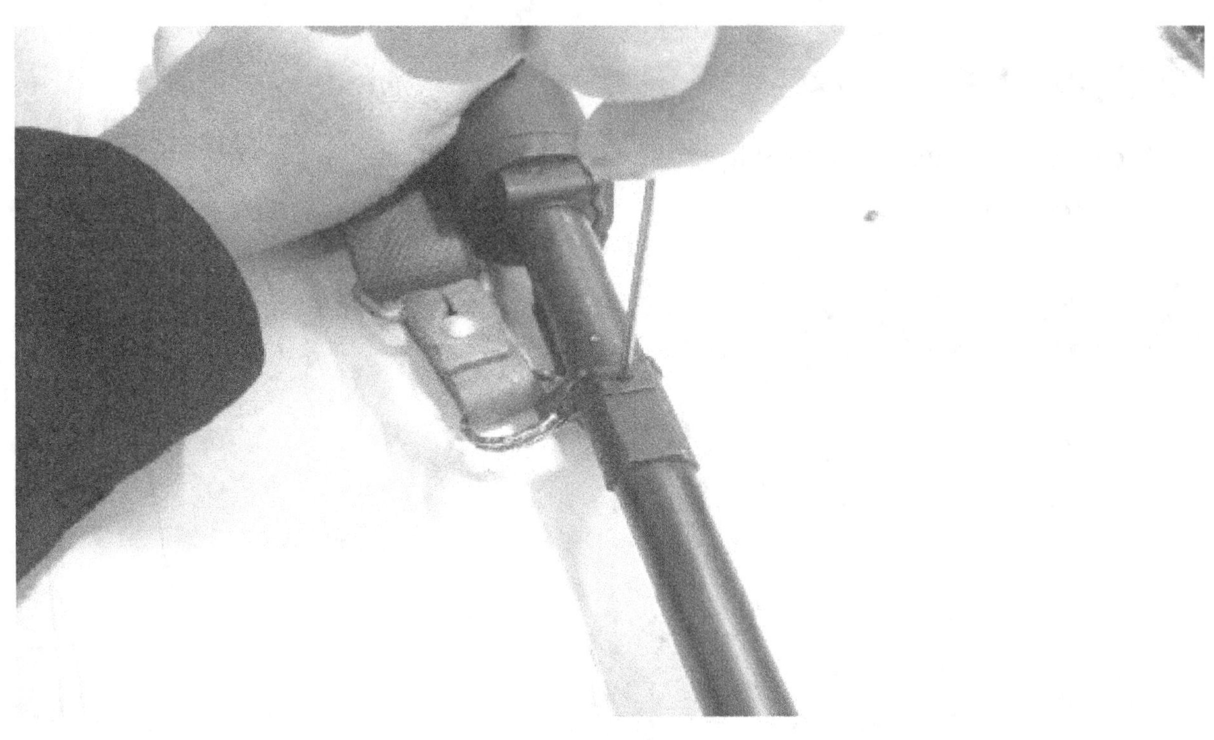

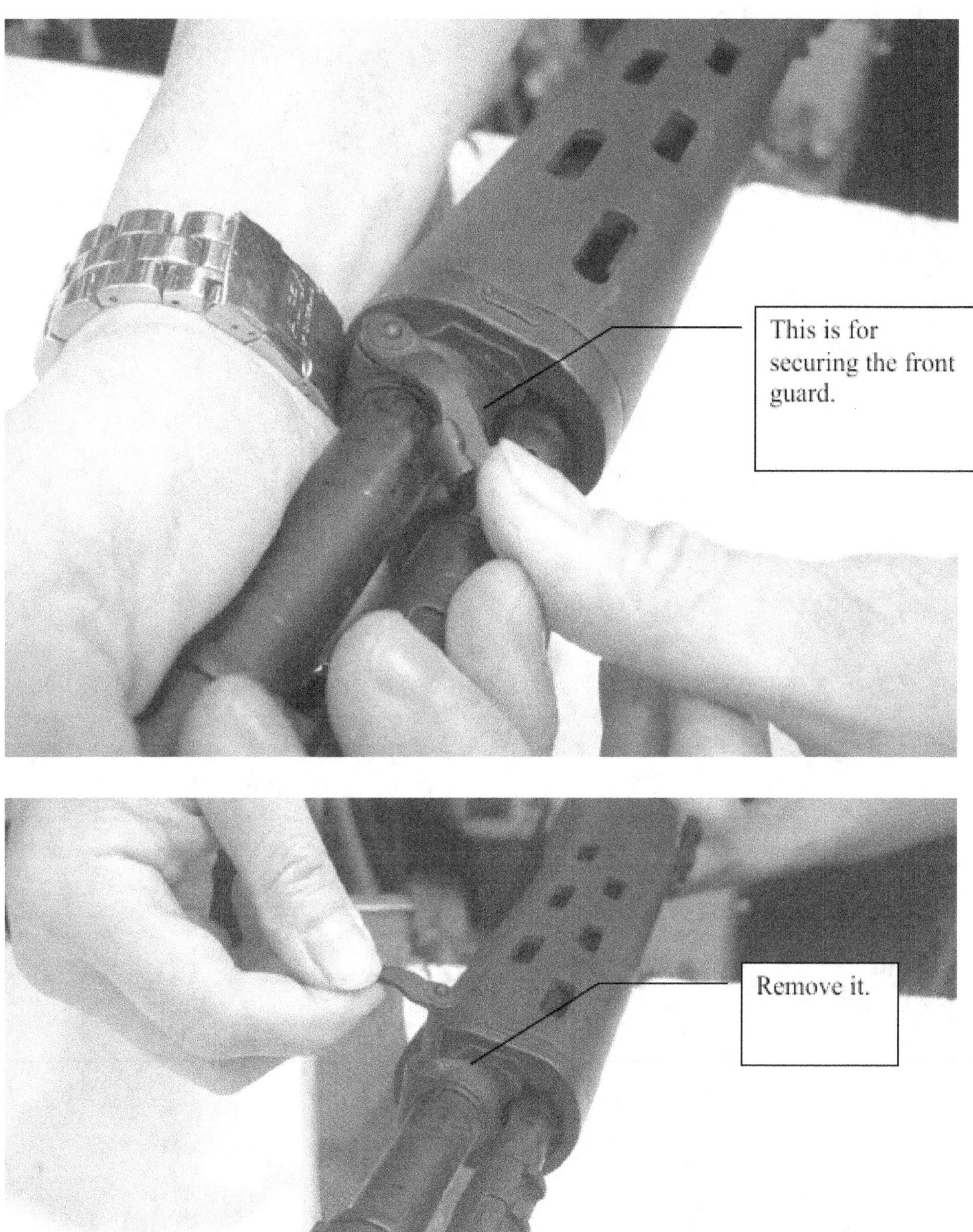

This is for
securing the front
guard.
Remove it.

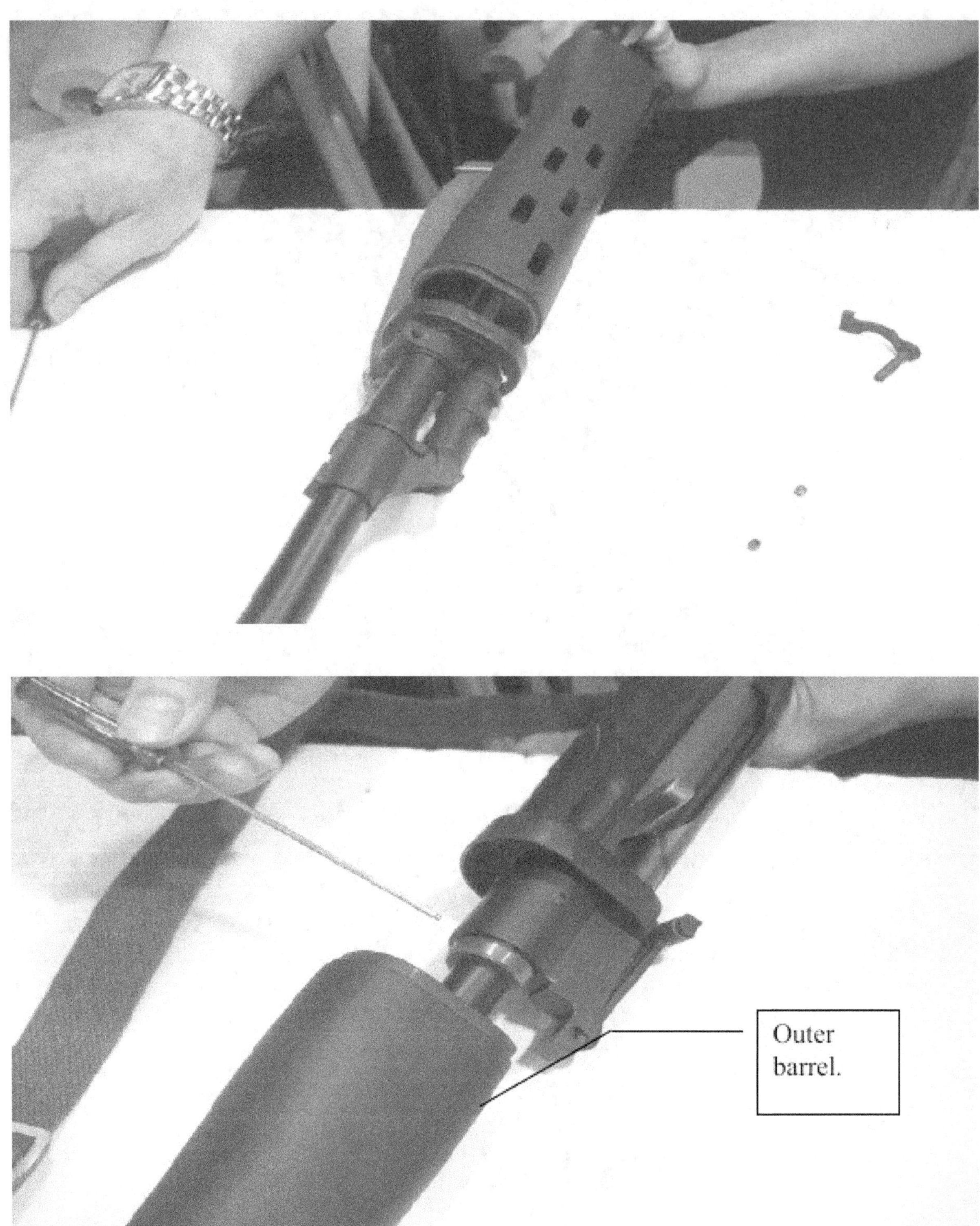
Outer
barrel.

THE MAG

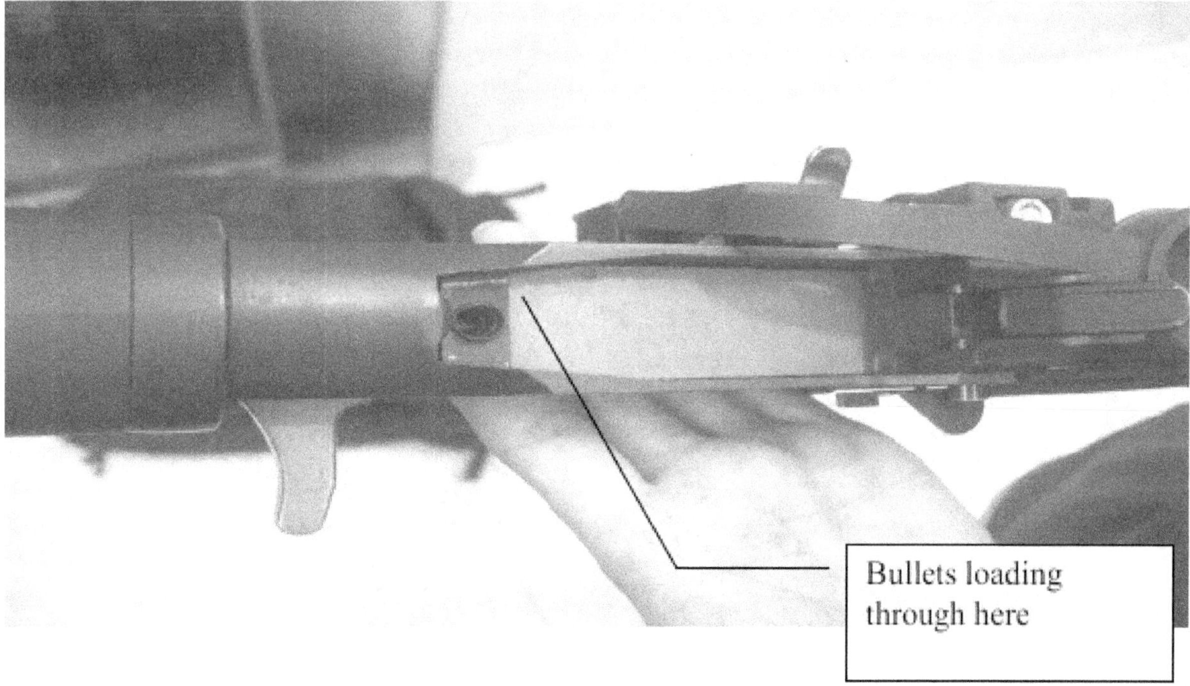

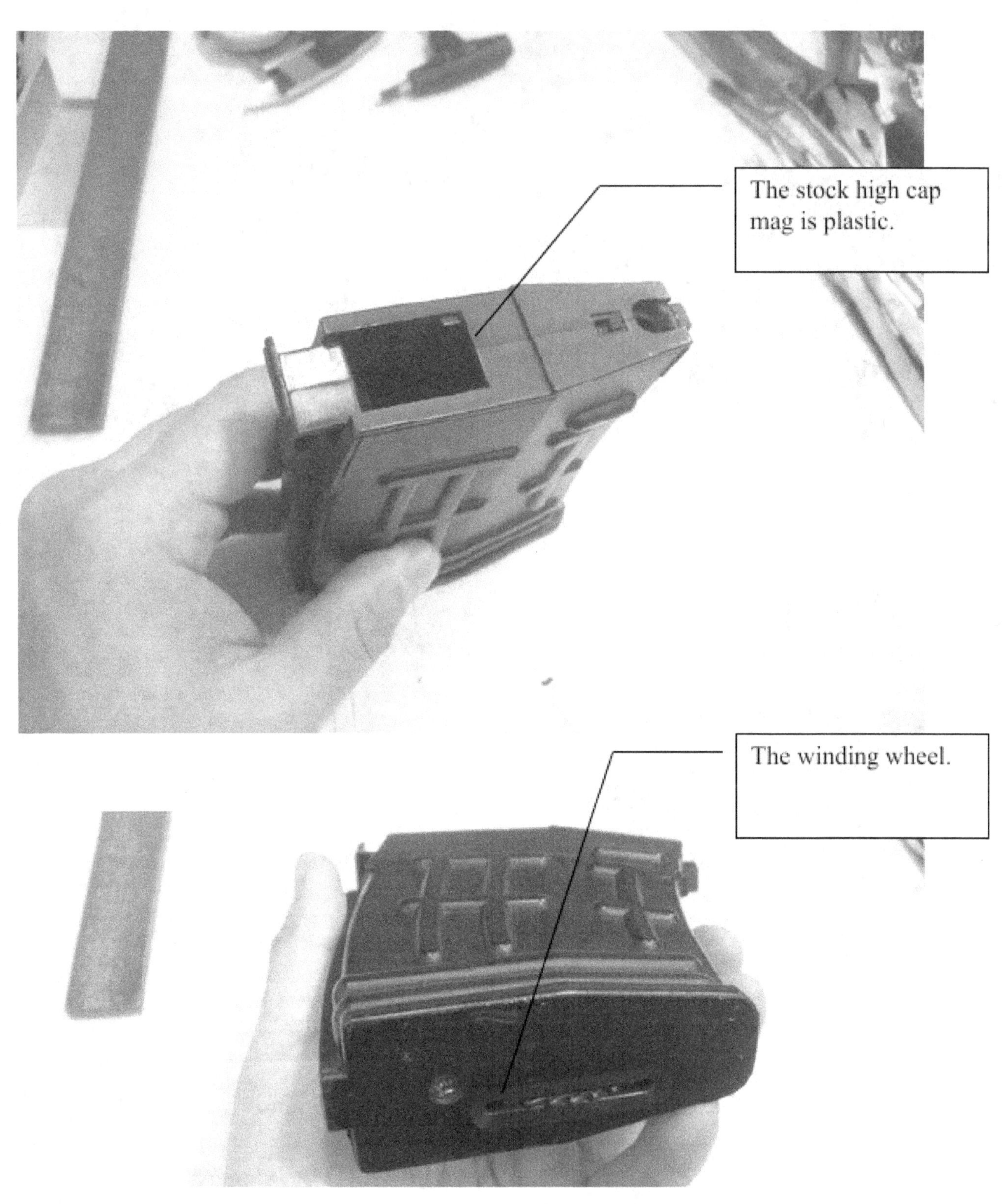

The stock high cap
mag is plastic.

The winding wheel.

THE BUTT AND THE GRIP

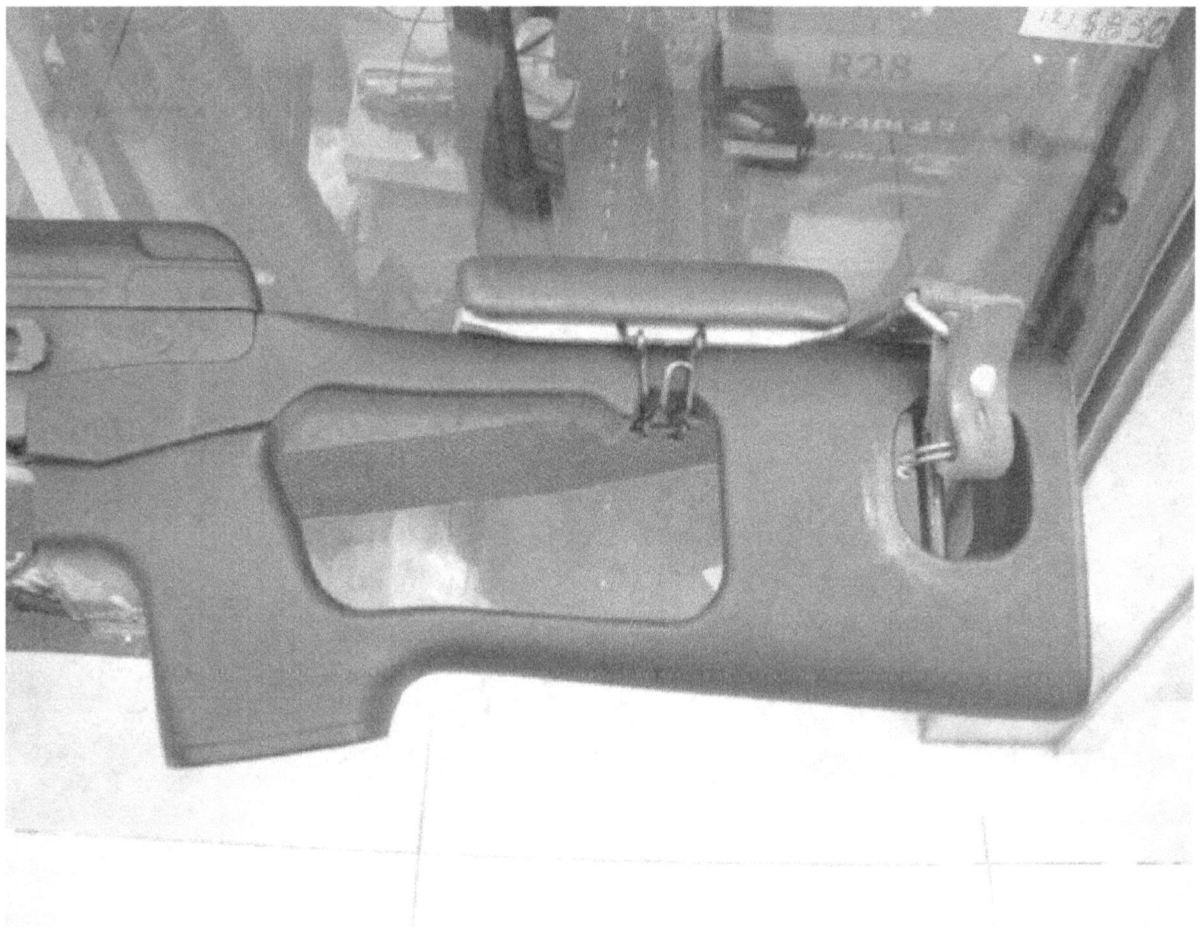

The butt and the grip are of a one-piece design. There are no critical parts housed inside.

REVIEW QUESTIONS AND ANSWERS

Question 1:

Refer to the photo below:

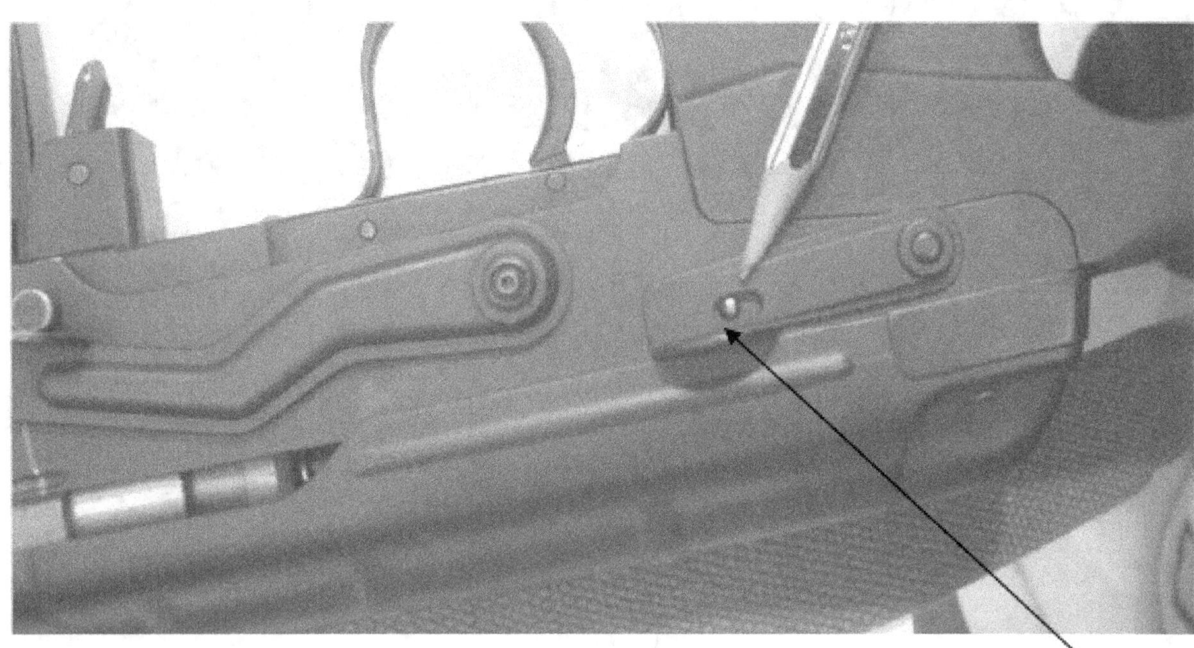

What is this component for?

A. securing the barrel
B. securing the top cover
C. securing the select fire
D. securing the hopup
E. None of the choices are correct.

Question 2:

Refer to the photo below:

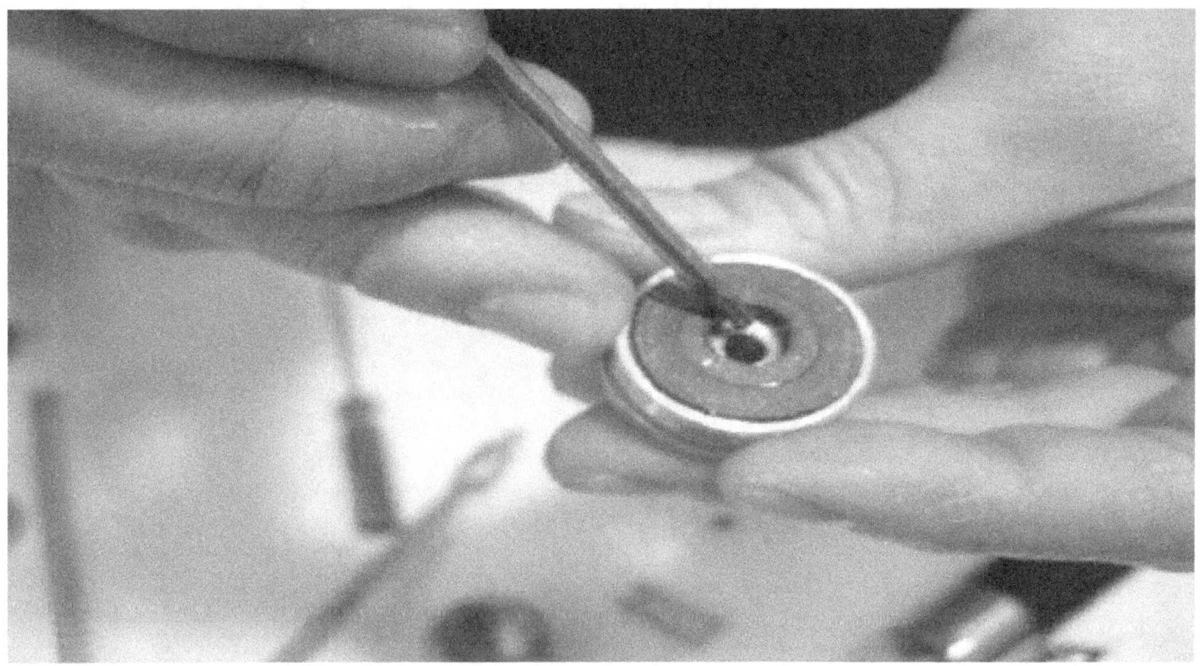

What component is this?

A. sector head
B. bevel head
C. cylinder head
D. piston head
E. None of the choices are correct.

Question 3:

What is the first defense against air leak?

A. the hopup chamber
B. the cylinder head pad
C. the piston head O ring
D. the spring guide
E. None of the choices are correct.

Question 4:

Refer to the photo below:

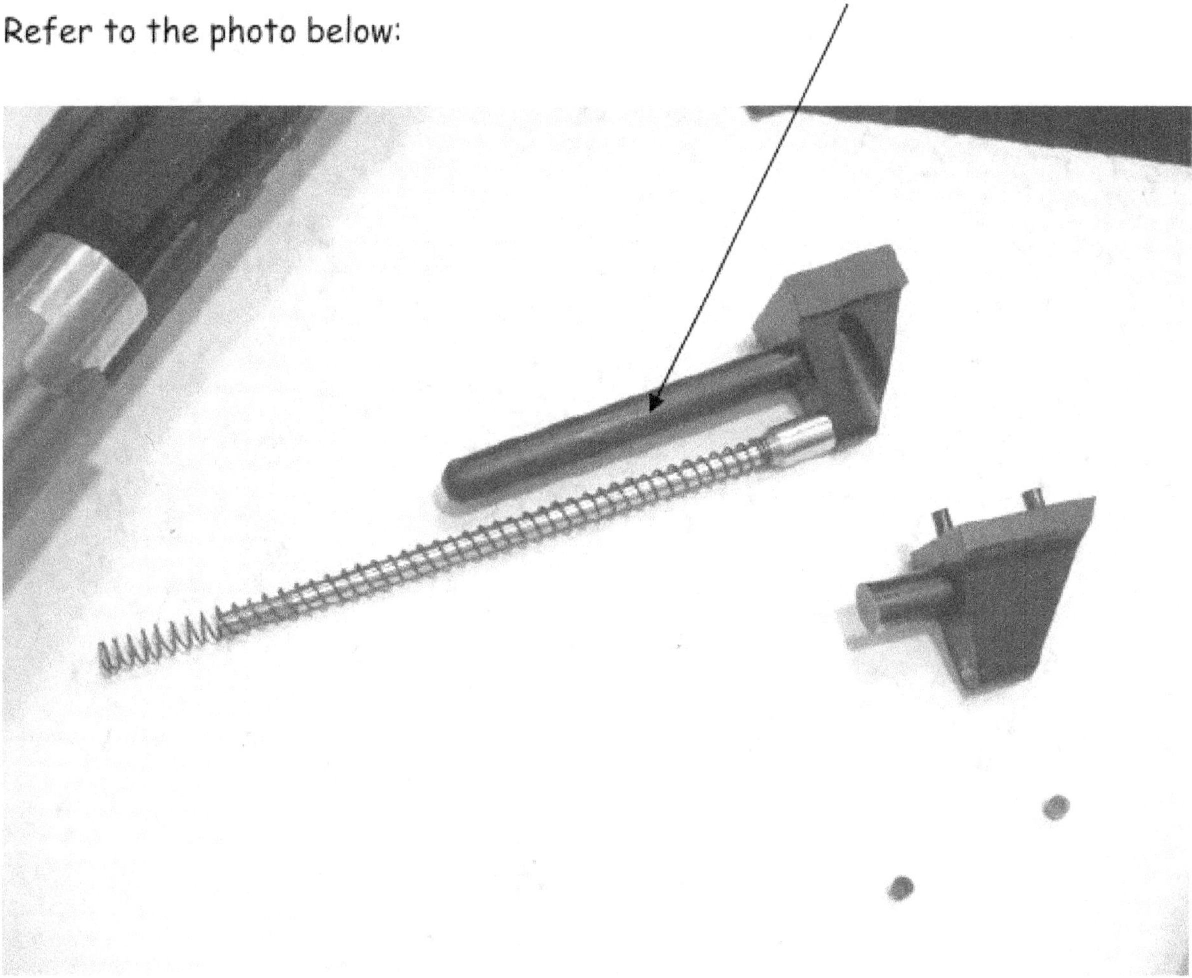

The highlighted component is for:

A. hopup release
B. safety switch
C. select fire
D. spring guiding
E. gas charging
F. None of the choices are correct.

Question 5:

Refer to the photo below:

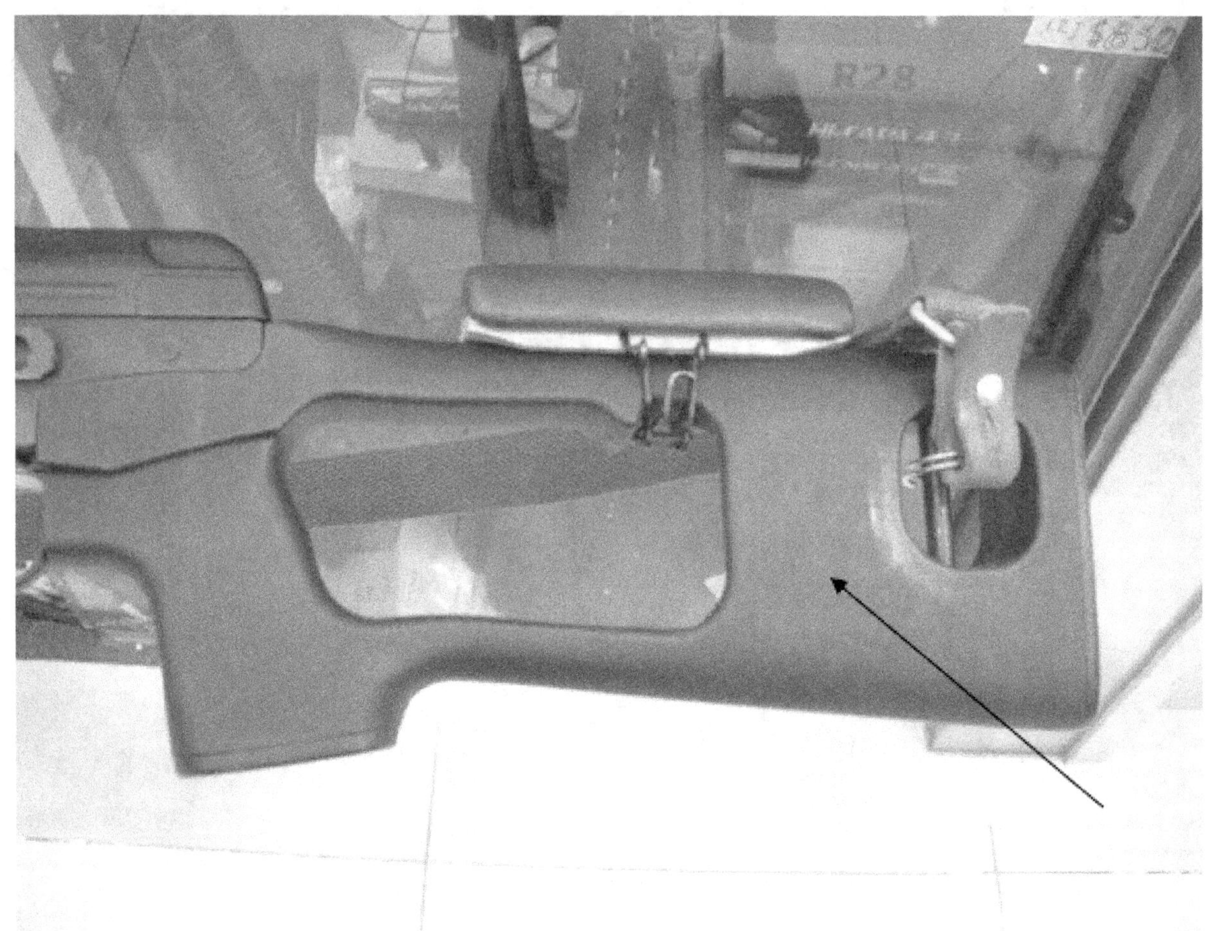

What important internal parts are kept inside the butt?

A. safety
B. select fire
C. mag drop
D. hopup adjustment
E. CO2 cartridge
F. None of the choices are correct.

<u>Answers</u>

1. B
2. C
3. C
4. D
5. F

CONCLUSION

Thank you for completing this self paced training module. The module gives you a clear and concise introduction to the different performance upgrade elements of the SVD rifle.

For latest product releases, updates and other free resources such as tech tips and InfoAPPS, please visit **http://airsoftpress.com**

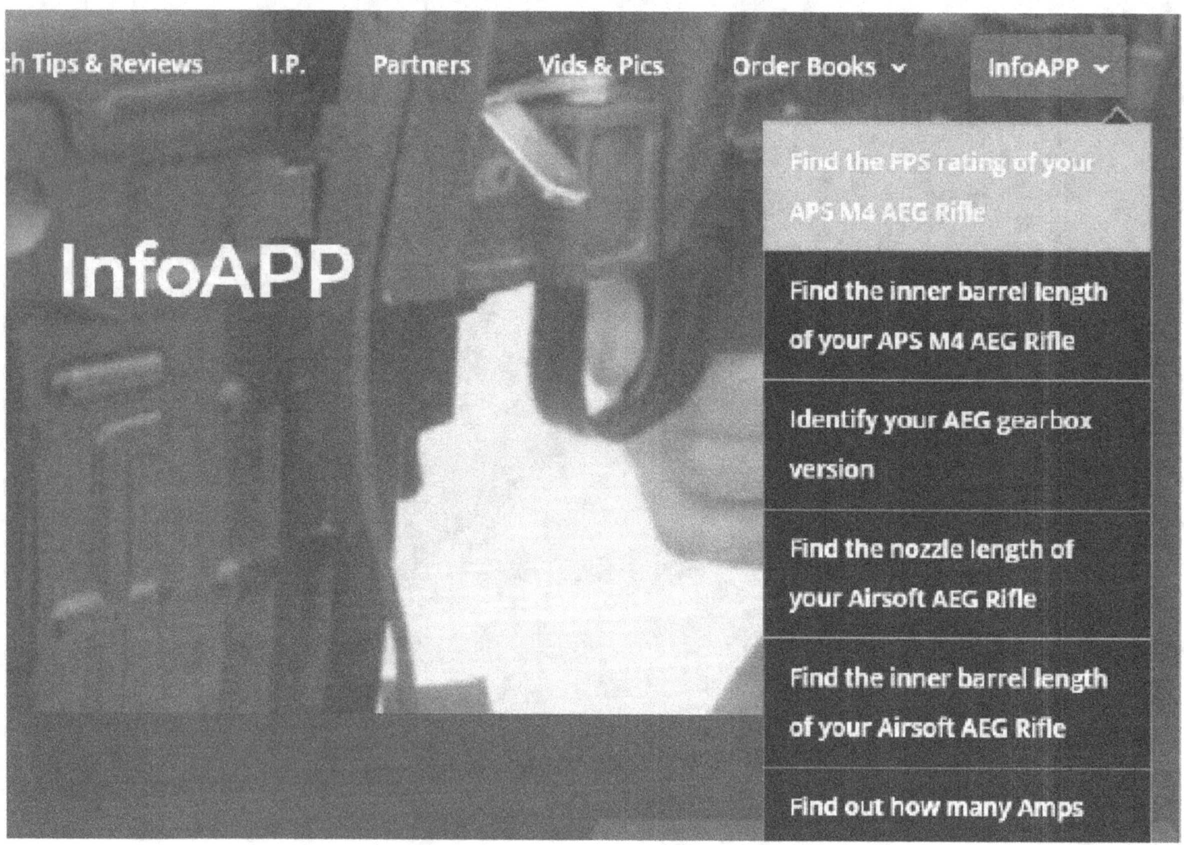

Please email your questions and comments to editor@airsoftpress.com.

Thank you.

　　AirsoftPRESS (Hong Kong).